Federalism: A Very Short Introduction

VERY SHORT INTRODUCTIONS are for anyone wanting a stimulating and accessible way into a new subject. They are written by experts, and have been translated into more than 45 different languages.

The series began in 1995, and now covers a wide variety of topics in every discipline. The VSI library currently contains over 550 volumes—a Very Short Introduction to everything from Psychology and Philosophy of Science to American History and Relativity—and continues to grow in every subject area.

Very Short Introductions available now:

For more information visit our web site

www.oup.com/vsi/

Mark J. Rozell
Clyde Wilcox

FEDERALISM

A Very Short Introduction

OXFORD
UNIVERSITY PRESS

OXFORD
UNIVERSITY PRESS

Oxford University Press is a department of the University of Oxford.
It furthers the University's objective of excellence in research, scholarship,
and education by publishing worldwide. Oxford is a registered trade mark of
Oxford University Press in the UK and certain other countries.

Published in the United States of America by Oxford University Press
198 Madison Avenue, New York, NY 10016, United States of America.

Library of Congress Control Number: 2019948074

ISBN: 978-0-19-090005-2

1 3 5 7 9 8 6 4 2

Printed in Great Britain
by Ashford Colour Press Ltd., Gosport, Hants.

In memory of our friend and collaborator, Ted G. Jelen

Contents

List of illustrations

Acknowledgments

We benefited from the very able research assistance of Piper Biery, Michelle Buehlmann, David Kanos and Hannah Lutz (George Mason University), and Louis Dezeran and Christopher Schorr (Georgetown University). Colleagues Uday Chandra and M. Reza Pirbhai offered helpful suggestions. David Lampo assisted with proofreading. Series editor Nancy Toff and editorial assistant Lena Rubin provided much guidance and outstanding editing as we developed this manuscript.

Over the past three decades we have lectured about the US federal system to thousands of groups of international visitors as a part of their US State Department–sponsored programs and have presented on this topic abroad numerous times as well. From these interactions we have learned much about how federalism operates around the world. Time and again, the international visitors and groups abroad have asked us to recommend a short primer on federalism that expands on what they learned from our lectures. This book is in response to those requests.

Preface

Federalism is the political system in which subnational units have some autonomy and authority and where there is power sharing between a national government and its subnational units. A federal system is one of three distinctive types among nations. In the unitary system, a central government has predominant control and delegates some responsibilities to the subnational units. In the confederate system, the subnational units are largely independent, sovereign units that hold the principle authority, whereas the national government is weak and possesses little or no controlling power over the subunits. In the federal system, overlapping and shared powers generally exist between the national and subnational units, and there are also distinctive areas of authority that belong uniquely to each unit. Not all federal systems distribute the powers and responsibilities of the different levels of government in the same way.

Our focus is the US federal system, in a comparative perspective. Although there are precedents in the Native American Indian nations and in the Swiss cantons, the United States was the first large-scale federal experiment and has the longest standing federal constitution. As such, it has served as a model or starting point for those who designed other federal systems.

Over the past three decades, each of us has given thousands of lectures about federalism in the United States to international visitors. The visitors attend these lectures as part of the US State Department's International Visitor Leadership Program, which funds young and mid-career professionals, emerging leaders, and top policy experts from around the world to spend from one to three weeks on a study tour of the United States. These programs generally focus on a single issue—the environment, historical preservation, or youth recreation programs, for example—but all groups receive a *federalism briefing* in the first day or two of their tour. After spending several days in Washington, DC, learning about national governments, the visitors travel to other parts of the country to experience the very different practices of states and local governments, as well as the varied cultures and social norms in diverse parts of the country.

Most visitors come to the United States with a common vision of how the country's political system operates. That vision, not surprisingly, is of a centrally dominated government in which almost all important decisions emanate from Washington, DC, and especially from the White House. To many of the visitors, to paraphrase the noted political scientist Charles O. Jones, the president is the presidency, the presidency is the government, and the United States is a presidential system. Jones was dissuading this line of thinking, given the system of separated powers at the national level, and we also spend much time in our lectures dissuading the visitors of this vision, given the realities of the federal system in the United States. The visitors travel around the country to see the federalism system in action and come away with a very different understanding of the US government than when they started.

Many governments in the world have federal systems, and some of our visitors come from other federal systems. But all federal systems are unique, reflecting the vagaries of history, geography, and politics, and to fully understand American politics and policy, visitors must understand federalism, American style. In the longer programs, visitors go to several states to see how each state addresses the issue of their tour.

The international visitors on these tours learn much about the workings of the federal system that many US citizens, including those who study in our university programs, do not readily understand. For most US citizens as well, the focus of the political system is Washington, DC, and the White House. Media coverage of US politics also has an intensive focus on the presidency, and the way in which the media personify the institution of the presidency leaves the overriding impression that the president is the center of the US government. Scholarly work in the US government subfield in our discipline of political science has focused on national government, and much less is written and taught regarding the governments and politics of state and local entities than about the presidency, Congress, and the courts. The draw to the big national stage, with all its drama and major political stakes, is understandable. Moreover, the complicated ways in which various state governments differ and operate do not make for a simple narrative. But to know the nature and operations of the US governmental system requires a clear understanding of the federal structure and how it works.

Chapter 1
American federalism in comparative perspective

On May 25, 1787, delegates from the thirteen American states convened in Philadelphia, charged with revising the Articles of Confederation that provided the governing framework for the country. Under the Articles of Confederation, each state remained sovereign, with only limited powers—principally in foreign policy—given to a central government. Each state was equal in the Congress and could veto legislation, and there was no executive power, although the Congress appointed an officer called a president to perform limited administrative duties. For funding, the Congress could only ask the states for money, having no power to tax after Rhode Island vetoed a national tariff. States habitually failed to provide all of the requested funds.

Instead of modifying the Articles of Confederation, the delegates drafted a new constitution that replaced the confederation with a federal form of government. During the nearly four months of deliberations, there was no ready consensus on which powers to grant the national and state governments. The final draft created a more powerful national government with powers to declare war, negotiate treaties, raise a permanent navy, raise revenue, regulate interstate commerce, and more generally (and vaguely) provide for the public welfare. States retained considerable sovereignty, including the right to set their own criminal law, civil law, and business regulations and to collect their own taxes.

Today, more than 230 years and one civil war later, the debate over which level of government should set which policies is far from settled. Politicians and interest groups often take strategic positions, proposing to address an issue at the level of government where they think they are most likely to win. Less commonly there are principled positions, based either on which level of government is best able to implement policies or on which level of government was initially intended to deal with the issue in 1787. Several key contemporary issues illustrate the challenges posed by federalism.

- *Same-sex marriage*: States regulate marriage and divorce, but the national government protects basic human rights including equality before the law. In 1967, the US Supreme Court overturned state laws barring interracial marriage in *Loving v. Virginia*. Although a ban on interracial marriage was part of the state constitution in Alabama until 2000, it was unenforceable. Between 2008 and 2015, both sides contested policy at the state level and some states allowed same-sex couples the right to marry. Others adopted amendments to their state's constitution not only barring same-sex marriage, but also barring their state from recognizing same-sex marriages performed in other states. Both sides also pursued national solutions, with conservatives unsuccessfully seeking a constitutional amendment limiting marriage to opposite-sex couples and liberals seeking a ruling by the Supreme Court allowing same-sex couples to marry. In 2015, the US Supreme Court declared that the fundamental right to marry is guaranteed to same-sex couples. Conservative states have responded by adopting laws that allow state and local officials to refuse to certify or perform marriages that violate the officials' religious values and to permit businesses specializing in wedding services to refuse to provide services to same-sex couples.
- *Abortion*: States regulate the health and safety of their citizens, but the national government protects human rights. In the 1960s, several states eased access to or fully legalized abortion. But in 1973, the US Supreme Court struck down most national, state,

and local abortion laws as violating women's privacy rights, thereby mandating a national policy on abortion. Since that time, antiabortion forces have attempted to win at the national level by amending the Constitution to ban abortion and by packing the Supreme Court with anti–abortion rights justices to reverse the ruling. Conservatives have succeeded at convincing some states to pass a variety of intrusive regulations, including mandating waiting periods and paternal consent laws and requiring that doctors warn women that abortions cause breast cancer (a view not shared by any medical association), requiring that women see an ultrasound image of the fetus, banning abortions performed in state hospitals, and requiring that even early, chemical abortions be performed in clinics with full emergency-care facilities. Though some states try to make it harder to obtain abortions, others, such as California, make it easier by paying for abortions for poor women with state funds.

- *Gun control*: Advocates for strict gun-control laws tend to turn to the federal government, hoping to create nationally uniform laws. Opponents prefer that the states continue to have the discretion to determine what policy approach best suits local circumstances. Federal action has been hard to achieve, even in the face of numerous mass shootings. In the states, policies vary substantially. For example, sixteen states ban carrying a concealed weapon on a college campus, ten states allow concealed weapons on college campuses, and twenty-three states allow colleges and universities to set their own policies. After a horrific mass shooting in a Florida high school in 2018, as efforts at the federal level stalled, activists pushed state governments to enact restrictions. Many took up the call and passed various restrictions on certain types of weapons or raised the age for the legal purchase of firearms.

- *Marijuana legalization*: Federal criminal law takes precedence over state law, but states regulate the health and safety of citizens. For many years, federal law has banned the sale and distribution of marijuana. But in 1996, California voted to allow for the use of marijuana to treat patients with certain ailments, and other states followed suit. These state actions created a conflict between federal and state law, and although the George W. Bush administration later prosecuted a few individuals in California, the Barack Obama administration instructed the Justice Department not to prosecute people distributing or using medical marijuana if it was consistent with state law. In 2012, Colorado and Washington legalized marijuana for adult recreational use. Today, more than thirty states allow for medical marijuana, and nine allow for recreational marijuana. The District of Columbia's approach is particularly complicated: a popular referendum supported legalization of use, but the district continues to criminalize buying or selling the drug. Thus, for example, a resident may buy a cheap T-shirt for the price of $50 and the shop owner includes a free "gift" as a thank you—a gram of marijuana. Some conservatives have pushed the Donald J. Trump administration to enforce national marijuana laws nationwide, whereas proponents of legal marijuana have sought to change the national law.

- *Voting rights*: States administer elections, including registering voters, but the national government protects human rights, including political rights. States can decide what hours their polls will be open and how and when voters can vote early. They can decide how citizens vote—by paper ballot, by voting machine, or even by mail-in ballot. They can decide how many precincts to put in which areas and what kinds of documents voters need to determine identity. In the 1960s, activists pursued laws and court cases to overturn various barriers to African American voting, including poll taxes, grandfather clauses, and literacy tests. More recently, in various states, Republicans passed a series of state laws that make it more difficult to vote, including limiting voting times and requiring various forms of identification. The political nature of these restrictions is evident in Texas, which requires a state-issued photo ID: the state does not honor state-issued student IDs, yet does honor gun licenses that do not contain photos. In Alabama, the state first required a photo ID issued by the Department of Motor Vehicles to vote and then closed thirty-one Department of Motor Vehicles offices in majority-black counties to make it harder for blacks to obtain the required voter ID. Opponents of these bills have challenged them in national courts with mixed success.

- *The environment*: The national government has the authority to ratify international treaties, but state and local governments cannot. Nonetheless, states may have domestic environmental laws that are stricter than national standards, and in some cases local governments have even stricter standards. National environmental laws apply throughout the country, but in recent years when Republicans have controlled the national government, environmentalists have focused on enacting better laws in states and cities, resulting in a tug of war between the federal government and subnational units. The Trump administration has pushed back in trying to prohibit states such as California from enacting automobile fuel standards that are tougher than the federal requirement. When the Trump administration withdrew the United States from the Paris Agreement to combat climate change, environmental activists quickly moved to influence subnational governments. Twenty state governments and more than fifty cities have pledged to abide by the agreement by adopting their own environmental laws in compliance with the standards of the Paris Agreement.

There is a dilemma that confronts all nations. On the one hand, uniform policies across the land can create equality for citizens, no matter where they live. On the other hand, different regions may have distinctive needs, capacities, values, and policy preferences. Although there are many variations, there are three types of solutions to the dilemma: unitary systems, confederations, and federal systems.

Unitary systems set most laws and policies at the national level. Some have only two levels of government: national government and local governments, such as cities and counties. Others have some kind of larger subnational government—states, regions, provinces—but they have no autonomous political power and merely enforce the laws passed by the national government. France, Japan, Israel, and Ghana are all examples of unitary political systems. In these countries, the national government makes final policy decisions on nearly all of the important matters, from defense and taxation to policing and education. Local governments may have some autonomy, but their decisions can be overruled by the national government.

Unitary governments face the problem of applying national standards to local units with differing needs, values, and cultures. In some unitary systems, certain kinds of decisions are left to local governments. In Japan, for example, local governments can adopt various types of education curricula from a list provided by the national government. The Tokyo prefecture has adopted a history textbook that is controversial for its treatment of the history of World War II. Japanese local governments also can adopt certain types of criminal laws. But in general, unitary governments set most laws and policies at the national level.

Confederations, by contrast, are loose coalitions of sovereign states that combine to share various tasks such as national defense, building roads, and other matters that the states agree to delegate to the national government. In many cases, regional governments can veto national laws or invalidate them within their borders.

Confederations face problems setting national standards and coordinating policy. After the Americans declared independence from Great Britain, they adopted a confederate-style system of government under the Articles of Confederation (adopted in 1781). Under that system, the national government was subservient to the states and it had no authority to levy taxes or impose laws on the states. During the Civil War, the Southern states that seceded from the union formed the Confederate States of America. The decentralization of the Confederacy was a great hindrance in the

1. During the Civil War, the Union regarded the Confederate states as "traitors." President Abraham Lincoln commanded federal armies to force several Southern states, which had seceded, back into the Union.

war, because the Confederate government could not tax the states, nor could it reallocate military supplies between states with surpluses and states with shortages. When Georgia threatened to secede from the Confederacy itself, president Jefferson Davis declared, "If the Confederacy fails, there should be written on its tombstone: Died of a Theory."

Today, there are no pure confederations in existence, but several countries, such as Switzerland and the European Union, have elements of confederation. The United Arab Emirates is a confederation of seven emirates, or kingdoms, although it also has elements of a federal system. Dubai and Abu Dhabi are the largest of these emirates and have more power as a function of size and wealth. Each emirate has its own hereditary emir, or king.

Federal systems generally have three layers of government—national, regional, and local. In federal systems, there is significant power sharing between national and regional governments and often with local governments as well. In federal systems, regions have their own governments and are able to exercise complete authority in some policy areas and shared authority with the national government in others.

Most large or populous nations are in some way federal—Australia, Brazil, Mexico, Nigeria, India, Canada, Germany, and Russia are all federal systems, for example. Federal systems are also more common in smaller countries with ethnic, national, or linguistic divisions, such as Malaysia and Belgium. In the past few decades, a number of countries have decentralized important policy areas, although they have not become fully federal polities. The principle of subsidiarity has been a rallying cry in many nations where distinctive linguistic, religious, or ethnic groups seek more autonomy from a central government.

The concept of devolution describes when a central government provides more autonomy and control to subnational units. In such cases, the central government may choose later to take back such powers. That is different from federalism, in which the respective powers of the national and subnational units are constitutionally defined.

Variations in federal systems

Every federal system is unique, but all face several common challenges. Federal nations have created differing solutions, based on their own unique national histories, cultures, and politics.

The number and size of regional subnational units vary widely. In many countries, the number of regional governments is based on historic precedents, reflecting long-standing borders, but some countries, such as Nigeria and India, have recently redrawn state boundaries and increased the number of states. The United States began with thirteen states, and this number grew as the country expanded westward by displacing native peoples.

Today, the United States has fifty states (and one federal capital district) that vary widely in size; Alaska, for example, is 548 times the geographical size of Rhode Island. The states differ substantially in population as well, from California, with nearly 40 million, to Wyoming, with slightly more than half a million. To put this in perspective, if everyone in Wyoming were to move to California and form a new city, five existing cities in California would be larger than the newly formed one. States are divided into counties as local units of governance, and these counties vary significantly in size as well. Some of the United States' more than three thousand counties include merely several thousand citizens, whereas others have populations of more than a million.

Only Russia has more subnational governments than the United States. India, Switzerland, Argentina, Mexico, and the European Union have between twenty-three and thirty-five, and South Africa, Austria, Canada, and Ethiopia have ten or fewer. Belgium has three regions and three cultural communities, reflecting the deep linguistic cleavages in that country. Other countries' subnational units also have wide variations in size and population. In India, the population of Uttar Pradesh is 307 times that of Sikkim.

Regional governments are represented in national governments in a variety of ways. In the United States originally, state governments selected their two senators for the upper chamber of Congress, but since the passage of a constitutional amendment in 1913, senators have been directly elected by the voters. The US Senate has two members from each state and is a coequal body with the House of Representatives. Outside these formal bodies, each state has established a lobbying presence in Washington, DC, to push for additional appropriations. In Germany, state governments are represented in the Bundesrat, which has veto power over all legislation that affects the Länder (states). In several other countries, the upper chamber of a bicameral parliament represents regional governments, but this chamber usually has limited powers.

Cleavages between and among the subnational units often pose significant challenges for maintaining stable federal systems. In the United States there are comparatively fewer ethnic, religious, and linguistic divisions among the states. No state is a particular ethnic group's homeland, and no state has a different official language or religion. Although the United States fought a bloody civil war in the 1860s, the country has fewer regional grievances than Spain or Nigeria. In many countries, regional governments reflect different ethnic or linguistic groups, and the regions or states may have been independent countries in the past. In Spain, the autonomous region of Catalonia has had a period of independence and was, for a time, a region of France. Many residents speak the Catalan language and fly the flag of Catalonia. In 2017, the region held an unauthorized referendum in which a majority of the voters supported independence from Spain, but the Spanish government did not recognize the referendum as legitimate and binding. In Nigeria, British colonials divided the country into three regions, which corresponded to the three largest ethnic groups. After a protracted civil war in the 1960s, the country sought to create states that spanned tribal and religious lines. Today, there are thirty-six states in Nigeria.

The extent to which the powers and responsibilities of subnational units are equal or identical may vary. The United States has symmetrical federalism, which means that all states, regardless of size and resources, have the same powers and the same responsibilities. Countries with regions with sizable linguistic, religious, or ethnic minorities frequently have asymmetrical federalism. In Canada, the predominantly French-speaking province of Quebec is recognized by the federal government as a distinct society and has its own legislative assembly and a lieutenant governor who serves as its head of state. In Spain, regional governments can opt out of some powers, such as education, and two regions collect all national taxes and then pay a fee to the national government for the services it administers. In Malaysia, two provinces in Borneo have special autonomy to protect their non-Malay cultures.

The source and sharing of revenues differ significantly in federal systems. In the United States, national, state, and local governments generally collect taxes separately, although in some states the state government collects local taxes and distributes the revenues back to the local governments. The national government collects more than 60 percent of total tax revenues and shares some of this revenue with state governments to achieve particular policy goals. The national government does not collect revenue from state governments, but instead taxes individual income, corporate income, imported goods, and the sale of a narrow set of items, such as gasoline, tobacco, alcohol, and diamonds. There is no explicit policy of equalization, but in practice there is some redistribution from wealthy states to poor states, primarily through a handful of programs such as Medicaid that provide benefits to poor citizens.

In Nigeria, the national government controls revenues, which are primarily generated by the sale of oil, and distributes money to the states. In Germany, the national and the Länder governments both collect taxes. The national government distributes funds to the Länder for various purposes, including administering national laws, but an explicit equalization program gives more money to poorer Länder. This practice was especially true during reunification, when the new Länder from the former East Germany received significant additional funds to enable them to catch up to the rest of the country.

In federal systems, some powers may be reserved exclusively for the national governments and some exclusively for state governments, and in some cases powers are reserved for local governments. Other powers are concurrent, so that more than one level of government can address an issue at the same time. Shared powers exist where there must be an agreement between national and regional governments. Residual powers are those that are not specified in the constitution or law, but where one level of government is presumed to dominate by default.

In the United States, the exclusive powers of the national government are relatively limited. The national government declares war, ratifies treaties, and prints money. In many policy areas, both federal and state authorities have jurisdiction, including criminal law, regulation of business, taxation, education, and healthcare. But in many cases state governments have principal authority, for example, in education, which the national government influences through grants of funds to accomplish particular policy goals.

In most federal systems the national government has more exclusive powers, although there remain many areas of concurrent powers. This is the approach in Austria, Germany, Malaysia, India, and Mexico. Canada is unique in having a relatively narrow range of concurrent powers, such as agriculture, immigration, and pensions. Brazil and India have constitutionally protected powers for local governments as well as national and regional governments. In the United States and many other federations, powers not specifically granted to the federal government reside with regional governments, but in Canada and some other systems, residual powers remain with the national government.

The US federal system is multilayered, multifaceted, and complex compared to most federal systems in the world. Although much of the focus of citizens, media, and educators is on the national political scene, most of the decisions that have the most profound effects on the day-to-day lives of Americans happen in state and local governments. Undeniably, however, for those who follow US government and politics, the national system not only may seem the most alluring, but also is far easier to comprehend than a multilayered federal system with more than ninety thousand governmental units. Among those units are not only states, counties, cities, and townships, but also water and land conservation boards, school boards, library boards, and many others. There are nearly thirteen thousand independent school districts alone in the United States. This system has evolved over time through custom, experimentation, law, and implementation.

Chapter 2
Federalism, American style

Federal systems are partially a function of history, geography, and political and social factors. The US federal system is more decentralized than that of most other countries, in part because thirteen separate colonies had spent years resisting central control from Britain and had finally fought a war of independence. These colonies had their own charters, their own taxes and printed money, their own economic and criminal laws, and their own police, jails, firefighters, and schools. They were not keen to give up power to a central government.

The original European settlers to the Americas had escaped monarchical regimes that restricted the freedoms of their citizens and prohibited certain religious beliefs and practices. By necessity, settlers established local governing practices. As the population grew, communities formed and organized into shires and parishes, based on English models. Shires became counties and then municipalities developed over time. The leaders of these units made law, determined inheritance rights, collected taxes, issued land titles, supervised local militias, and took care of other governing details.

The development of a federal system therefore was very much a function of circumstances. The founders of the Republic did not invent federalism. There were tribal federations and confederations in the Middle East thousands of years earlier, and the Iroquois federation in North America dates to the mid-fifteenth century. But there were no detailed records of earlier federations, so the founders did not have any examples on which to model the US federal system.

Today, countries that are considering establishing federal structures often send experts to study federal systems such as those in Germany, Canada, and the United States. Indeed, the US State Department brings visitors to the United States from nations that are creating or considering federal systems to study what works (and what does not). The men and women who design new federal governments have an abundance of advice and information. But the founders of the American republic had neither. Instead, they had to rely on their experiences as subjects of the British crown and as citizens in colonies that had important self-governing powers.

The colonial period and the Articles of Confederation

During the colonial era, each colony had a government that had autonomy on many matters. The British permitted the colonial governments to create their own laws, as long as the acts did not directly contradict English law. They had their own governments, including elected legislatures. This degree of local autonomy was a necessity given slow communications at the time between the colonies and the British central government. In this regard, the origins of US federalism were a result of circumstances and necessity more than intentional design. The relationships between colonial towns, the colonies, and the British central government made the eventual transition to a system of intergovernmental relations in the new nation quite natural.

The American war for independence was a revolt against the authoritarian rule of the British Crown and its refusal to allow the colonists the most basic rights of British citizens, such as representation in Parliament. The colonial governments, and ultimately the Articles of Confederation (passed in 1781), established the principles of local governing sovereignty and opposition to centralization and strong executive power.

Although the Articles-of-Confederation form of government formally lasted for only eight years, it represented the preferences of the delegates for self-governance and weak central government. The colonists saw themselves not so much as a part of a unified country, but more as a collection of independent countries joined together in a loose alliance. There was no national consciousness, as we understand it today. Although the war for independence fostered a sense of unity, it did not build a sense of nationhood. The men who created the Articles of Confederation equated centralized power with tyranny.

It is telling that when those who founded the republic declared independence and thus had their first opportunity to establish an independent governing system, they opted for decentralized authority. Under the Articles of Confederation, the national government was merely a congress of the states with no formal executive power or national judicial system. Executive and judicial functions resided solely with the states. The national government possessed no authority to enforce its own laws, regulate commerce, or even raise a national army without the consent of the states.

The states were independent sovereign entities, and citizens often referred to their state as their *nation*. At the time, citizens emphasized the differences among the colonies and were suspicious of each other. Although the articles established at the outset that "the stile of this confederacy shall be 'The United States of America,'" among the colonists there was more a sense of separatism among the states than unity.

The one unifying element was the war for national independence. But this unity of purpose to unburden the colonies of British control did not translate into a belief in any alternative system of central government control. Indeed, the second article of the document established the central role of the state governments: "Each state retains its sovereignty, freedom and independence, and every power, jurisdiction, and right, which is not by this Confederation expressly delegated to the United States, in Congress Assembled."

The Articles of Confederation provided that the national Congress, not the states, would handle matters of war, alliances, embassies, and foreign affairs generally and that it would pay for the nation's common defense. Yet the states could override any national action, and the national government was dependent on the states for actual funding. The national government had no mechanism to enforce any of its actions on the states or to ensure that the states cooperate with each other. With a complete lack of unity and states generally suspicious of each other, there were substantial internal government debts, and some states overprinted their currencies in response. States had trade wars with each other, and the national government had no real ability to support a system of national defense. These failures, among others, led to a call for a constitutional convention for the purpose of amending or improving the Articles of Confederation.

The new Constitution

The 1787 convention in Philadelphia quickly moved beyond its initial mandate, as the delegates recognized that the situation required a more substantial change than a mere revision of the existing form. Most delegates believed that the needs of the states could be met only with a stronger national government, but there was disagreement about just how strong that government should be or how it should be formed. Hence, delegate James Madison introduced his Virginia Plan—a proposal to create a large federal republican government—and the majority of the convention delegation determined that instead of the unanimous consent required to amend the Articles of Confederation, a new constitution would require ratification by only nine of the states. Yet the delegates did not have a unified view of what the new government structure should look like. Delegates were divided between two concepts: nationalism and federalism, as these concepts were understood at the time.

Madison's proposal represented the nationalist view. The nationalists believed the Confederation had been too weak to provide for the defense, liberty, and general welfare of the individual states. They argued that to ensure these main objectives, there needed to be a supreme national government that had executive, judicial, and legislative powers. Such a national government would be better able to secure private rights and dispense justice.

The federalists, by contrast, believed that a strong national government would destroy personal liberties by leading ultimately to despotism. Their preference was to maintain a system of sovereign independent states that would govern themselves according to commonly shared local values and customs. A strong national government, they reasoned, would impose its will uniformly on the nation and thus eliminate the local autonomy and freedoms that were at the heart of the American quest for independence from British control of the colonies.

A few weeks into the convention, the federalists introduced an alternative to Madison's proposal—the New Jersey Plan. Although the convention rejected this alternative, many of its core principles were established in the new constitution ultimately proposed at the convention. For example, the New Jersey Plan proposed a system of power sharing, reserving some powers for the national government and others for the states. Also, it proposed a unicameral legislature in which each state possessed an equal number of votes in the Congress. The Virginia Plan had proposed a legislature composed of members from each state in proportion to the state's population size. The Connecticut Compromise adopted both principles, creating a bicameral legislature that protected the nationalist interests of representation for the people through the House of Representatives—who would be elected by the voting populace of a state—while seeking to protect the interests of the states in the Senate—where officials were originally selected by the state government. Under the Articles of Confederation, representatives served the interests of the states alone. Under the proposed constitution, representatives would protect the rights of the people as well as the interests of the individual states.

The federalists achieved protection of a number of key states' issues in the new Constitution. Among these were the powers of states to tax, to maintain a militia, and to make commercial decisions. For the Southern states, this also meant the right to maintain the institution of slavery. The Constitution prohibited Congress from abolishing the importation of slaves for twenty years and required the extradition of escaped slaves across state lines. For the purposes of representation in the House, it allowed Southern states to count slaves as three-fifths of a citizen, although those slaves had none of the rights of citizens. These compromises delayed but did not ultimately prevent the nation's bloody civil war in 1861–65.

Additionally, the Constitution contained key protections of states' powers in the federal structure of the government. Congress would be a bicameral body, with the House of Representatives apportioned within each state based on population, but the Senate was apportioned based on equal representation for each state. James Madison wrote of the House, "So far the government is *national, not federal.*" As to the Senate, he wrote, "So far the government is *federal, not national*" (*Federalist No. 39*). Although both houses are equal bodies, the Constitution gave the Senate, the repository of states' powers in the federal government, certain unique powers, such as confirming cabinet secretaries and federal judges by majority vote, as well as ratifying treaties by at least a two-thirds majority. Thus, if a president wants to sign a formal treaty with another nation-state, he must take into account not only broader national perspectives but also the more parochial interests represented by the states in the Senate to achieve ratification. With a two-thirds majority requirement, it is possible for a minority of small-population states representing a tiny portion of the overall national population to put a stop to a treaty.

The states administered elections. They conducted all federal elections within their boundaries as well as state and local elections. State legislatures chose members of an Electoral College, who then selected the president. Thus, presidential elections are about winning states rather than the national popular vote. Originally, the state governments also chose US senators.

Changing the form of government itself through a constitutional amendment requires the consent of at least two-thirds of each house of Congress and then three-quarters of the states. Again, an activated minority of states represented either in the Senate or in the state legislatures can prevent the enactment of any proposed amendment to the US Constitution. Moreover, the equal representation of states in the US Senate cannot be changed by amendment.

The nationalists ensured that the national government would have the power to tax—a key feature that was missing in the Articles of Confederation—raise a military, and regulate interstate and international commercial activity. In addition, the nationalists were able to ensure that the national government had the authority to "make all Laws which shall be necessary and proper for carrying into Execution the foregoing Powers, and all other Powers vested by this Constitution in the Government of the

United States, or in any Department or Officer thereof" (Article 1, Section 8, Clause 18).

In addition to containing more enumerated powers for the national government than the Articles of Confederation, the Constitution prohibited certain actions by the states. For example, Article 1, Section 10, forbids the states from creating their own alliances, establishing independent tariffs, or engaging in war "unless actually invaded, or in such imminent Danger as will not admit of delay." In addition, it preserved for the citizens of each state the same "privileges and immunities of Citizens in the several States," indicating that states cannot create laws or privileges that violate those existing in other states (Article 4, Section 2, Clause 1).

Ultimately, the proposed Constitution encapsulated both nationalist and federalist perspectives of government. It granted the national government power to direct foreign affairs, arbitrate between the states, and protect the interests of the union. Additionally, it preserved powers of the states to challenge the national government, to maintain their regional identities and economic systems, and to keep their militias.

The states needed to ratify the new Constitution, but only nine states were required to form the new government, a dramatic reduction from the unanimous consent required by the Articles of Confederation. In effect, by ratifying the Constitution, the states agreed to the creation of a large federal republic in which a national government would possess some significant powers over the states. Madison described the voluntary approval of the states as such: "Each State, in ratifying the Constitution, is considered as a sovereign body independent of all others, and only to be bound by its own voluntary act. In this relation, then, the new Constitution, if established, be a *federal* and not a *national* constitution" (*Federalist No. 39*). However, states or other

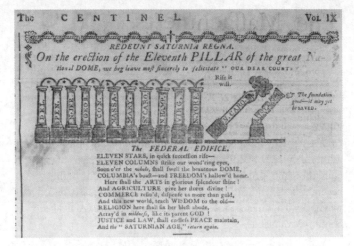

2. In July 1788, New York became the eleventh state to ratify the US Constitution. This woodcut in the *Massachusetts Centinel* celebrates "the eleventh pillar of the great national dome."

governmental subunits that enter into federal systems ultimately surrender their autonomy.

Not all colonists agreed with Madison's solution. After the convention a debate raged between the advocates and the opponents of the proposed Constitution. Alexander Hamilton, James Madison, and John Jay contributed a series of newspaper columns in defense of the Constitution, known to us collectively as *The Federalist*. In a twist of language, the proponents became known as the federalists and the opponents as the antifederalists. The federalists prevailed in convincing the states to ratify the document, and it went into effect in 1789. The United States has been governed continuously by the Constitution since.

The antifederalists made the case for what now would be called *states' rights*. They opposed the proposed constitution out of the fear that a large federal republic would ultimately become a central government-dominated system, leaving little or no freedom to the states to self-govern. In their view, the Constitution created a superior federal power and relegated the states to a secondary role.

Although the federalists are best known for having made the case for a stronger national government, they refuted the antifederalist claim that the states would be subservient to a powerful central authority. Indeed, Hamilton argued in *Federalist No. 16* that a strong national government is necessary to keep the states in harmony with each other—something that had been missing under the Articles of Confederation. In *Federalist No. 17*, he noted that the most common duties of government bodies of the time— civil and criminal laws and procedures—would be the purviews of the states, not the federal government, and thus the people would always retain their principal loyalties to their states.

Much of *The Federalist* indeed seeks to allay the concerns of those who feared a too-strong national government and a weakening of state-level government authority. Most directly, Madison assured critics that the new government would be both federal and national: "The proposed Constitution, therefore, is in strictness neither a national nor a federal Constitution but a composition of both. Its foundation is federal, not national; in the sources from which ordinary powers of the government are drawn, it is partly federal and partly national; in the operation of these powers, it is national, not federal; in the extent of them it is federal, not national; and in the authoritative mode of introducing amendments it neither wholly federal nor wholly national" (*Federalist No. 39*).

The federalists' argument simply was the stronger one overall, because the system under the Articles of Confederation was in disarray and there was no disputing the need for the unifying role of a stronger national government. The Constitution nonetheless made it clear that the powers of the national government were limited to certain core functions that only a national government is capable of performing competently: matters of war and peace, regulating interstate and international commerce, coining a common currency, protecting the public order, and taxation.

The major legacy of the antifederalists was the inclusion of a Bill of Rights as the first ten amendments to the US Constitution. The very fear of an excessively strong national government and its potential to undermine the rights and the liberties of the people, as well as the independent authority of the states, resulted in the demand by key opponents of the Constitution that the document contain a guarantee of the rights of the people. The Bill of Rights ultimately was the last compromise of the constitutional period, as the proponents of the document, who had initially resisted the idea of specifying the people's rights—assuming these were inferred in the Constitution—agreed as a unifying act to introduce in the first Congress a series of amendments. Among the key amendments was the First Amendment, which guaranteed freedom of speech, the press, religion, and assembly.

The Constitution specified certain enumerated powers of the national government and the duty of Congress to pass all laws "necessary and proper" to carry out those governmental functions. The Tenth Amendment to the Constitution made it clear, however, that all other powers would be reserved to the states and to the people, ensuring that the states would remain the principle authorities of local control: "The powers not delegated to the United States by the Constitution, nor prohibited by it to the States, are reserved to the States respectively, or to the people." This amendment was a critical concession to the antifederalists that the national power would be a limited one and that the states could continue to carry on their core functions unfettered by the national government.

The Constitution, state powers, and the Bill of Rights

The Constitution and the Bill of Rights set into motion the formal basis for the federal system of the United States. Key provisions of the Constitution specifically address how federalism would operate. For example, Article IV contains several requirements to ensure that the states would function in harmony with each other. Article IV, Section 1, provides that the states must accept and respect the "public acts, records, and judicial proceedings of every other state." Thus, a marriage license obtained in one's home state is a valid license anywhere in the United States, even though different states have different requirements, such as the legal age to marry. In the case of same-sex marriage, a basis for the Supreme Court decision to mandate marriage equality (*Obergefell v. Hodges*, 2015) was the refusal of several states to acknowledge the legal validity of same-sex marriages conducted in other states. Article IV also requires extradition across state borders of those accused of crimes to ensure that the laws of each state are respected, even by citizens of other states. Additionally, those accused of a crime in a state of nonresidency are afforded the same legal rights and privileges as any accused person who is a resident of the state where the alleged crime occurred. States may not discriminate against each other's citizens under their own laws.

States must honor contracts and civil judgments from other states. They are also required to give people who move to their state the same rights as the people who already live there. Thus, young people who move to a state and establish citizenship must be charged in-state tuition rates at public universities and colleges, even if their parents live in another state. And poor people who move to a state are entitled to that state's welfare benefits, even if the state from which they are moving paid lower benefits.

Finally, states may not enter into exclusive commercial compacts with one another without the permission of the federal government. Today, there are hundreds of such interstate compacts that the federal government has approved, and about two hundred are actively in force. Interstate compacts bind states to honor each other's drivers' licenses and also bind forty-five states that are signatories to an agreement to count traffic violations issued in another state against drivers in their home state. Other compacts are much narrower, such as the one between Pennsylvania and West Virginia to provide flood control for the Wheeling watershed.

The Constitution barred the states from certain actions that would create problems for the new nation. It barred states from printing their own money, taxing imports or exports, or entering into a treaty with another country. Most federal systems have adopted these limitations, although the cantons in Switzerland have the power to negotiate treaties with foreign nations.

Although US states cannot enter into treaties with other countries, they can enter into international trade relationships, as long as these relationships do not violate federal trade laws, and governors frequently travel to other countries to promote trade. The state of Texas maintains a sizable trade office in Mexico, and many states maintain trade offices in China, India, and other countries. States can also set their own domestic laws to comport with international treaties, and many states have done this with regard to environmental treaties that the United States has either failed to ratify or withdrawn from.

The national government is responsible for defending the states against foreign attack and domestic insurrection if the states request assistance. The national government can admit a new state to the union, but cannot merge or divide existing states without their approval. Only two states have divided in US history—when Maine separated from Massachusetts in 1820 and when West Virginia split off from Virginia during the Civil War and joined with the Union. Because Virginia had already seceded from the Union, its permission was not required to approve the admission of West Virginia into the Union.

The Constitution listed the powers that were given to the national government. Included in this list were various powers relating to foreign policy and military defense—the right to declare war, raise an army and a navy, call forth a militia, conduct trade with other nations, and negotiate and ratify treaties.

On the domestic front, the Constitution gave the national government the power of commerce—to print money, to borrow money, to collect taxes and duties, to punish counterfeiters, to build post offices and roads, and to regulate interstate commerce. When national laws are passed that are within the powers of the national government, they take precedence over any state law that would contradict them.

What is striking from a modern perspective is what is *not* on the list of national government functions—that is, the policy areas and powers that the national government was not given in the Constitution. In fact, much of what the national government currently tries to do involves activities that the Framers did not—and probably could not—envision. The Constitution gave the national government no explicit powers to build schools or develop a national education curriculum, and it did not create a right to a free public education. It did not explicitly give the national government the power to set environmental standards or to break up economic monopolies, regulate political parties, provide healthcare to the poor, or help to promote culture. It even reserved to the states the right to conduct elections. In the Tenth Amendment to the US Constitution, the founders specified that any powers not explicitly given to the national government were reserved to the states and the people.

Here, the national Constitution clearly shows its age. It was difficult in 1787 to imagine the national government, already burdened by the costs of the Revolutionary War and with few employees and poor funding, conducting national elections. There were not yet any political parties to regulate, no industrial factories polluting the water and air, and no large companies exercising monopoly power. It is likely that had the same men who drafted the original Constitution lived and met today, they would have specified a different list of powers for the national government.

The founders knew that they could not anticipate all circumstances in which the national government might need to act, so they added vague language that might allow the national government to deal with changing circumstances. The Constitution gave the Congress the power "to make all laws which shall be necessary and proper for carrying into execution the foregoing powers." This *necessary and proper clause* is sometimes called the *elastic clause* for the way it stretches national government power. Moreover, the Constitution charged the national government with spending money to promote the common defense and general welfare of the nation. This constitutional vagueness has allowed for important expansion of national power. But it also provides for ongoing debates and struggles over which level of government should control which policies.

Originally, the founders allowed Congress to provide for the general welfare, but only through its power to tax and spend. In the early days, many policymakers believed that the national government should use this power sparingly. In 1796, the government considered a request from Georgia for aid to Savannah, which was devastated by a fire on November 26. Two-thirds of the city was ruined, making it at the time the most destructive fire in American history. The fire destroyed over two hundred homes and buildings. Hundreds of dazed people wandered the streets, with their homes, their possessions, and often their means of livelihood gone.

Congress debated aid to Savannah on principled terms. All agreed that the city had suffered grievously, but the question was whether this was an issue best addressed by the national government. Many members of Congress argued that if relief were granted to Savannah, soon all kinds of cities would be requesting assistance. In the end, Congress declined to appropriate funds to rebuild the city or to provide relief to its residents. But today the national government provides funds to the fire department of Savannah to help it prepare for terrorist attacks and other potential disasters.

The Bill of Rights now supplements the US Constitution's requirements regarding federalism. That was not the intention of the founders of the Republic, because the Bill of Rights originally applied only to acts of the federal government. Citizens had no recourse to the Bill of Rights to protect themselves from violations or perceived violations of federally guaranteed rights by the states. The opponents of the Constitution, who feared an overbearing federal power, pushed for a bill of rights to protect citizens from the national government, while assuming that the states would be the natural repositories of peoples' rights. State governments also had bills of rights, presumably mitigating the need for any federal protections of people against actions of the states. Given that the founders established a dual federalism system, issues of citizen rights under the federal system and in the states were to remain within separate spheres.

The post–Civil War period saw the passage of three civil rights amendments to the US Constitution. Most important here, the Fourteenth Amendment stated, "No State shall make or enforce any law which shall abridge the privileges or immunities of citizens of life, liberty, or property, without due process of law; nor deny to any person within its jurisdiction the equal protection of the laws." Although it was widely acknowledged as a civil rights action to abolish slavery, some saw the Fourteenth Amendment as a means to protect the rights of citizens against actions of the states. Throughout the rest of the nineteenth century, federal court opinions generally upheld the original intent of the Bill of Rights as a protection only against federal actions. Beginning in the 1920s, decisions of the US Supreme Court began to interpret the Fourteenth Amendment as incorporating the Bill of Rights to include actions of the state governments.

The Bill of Rights currently is understood to protect citizens' federally guaranteed rights against the acts of all levels of government—federal, state, and local. The Fourteenth Amendment thus constituted a major shift in the constitutional understanding of the relationship between the federal government and the states. Its equal protection clause, that no state may deny any citizen under its jurisdiction "the equal protection of the laws," has resulted in landmark decisions such as the 1954 *Brown v. Board of Education*, in which a unanimous Supreme Court mandated that states may not maintain segregated public schools.

The Constitution establishes some basic ground rules for American federalism, but more than the details remained to be worked out. The founders, like Americans today, disagreed about the relative powers of national and state governments. Over the course of the nation's history, the basic assumptions about the balance of national and state powers have shifted and changed. In general, the power of the national government has grown dramatically over the past century, but more recently the Supreme Court has begun to rule on behalf of the states in some areas such as interstate commerce.

In the early decades of the new country, many of the leading founders disagreed about what the Constitution said about the balance of power between national and state governments. Thomas Jefferson, for example, believed that the national government was created by the states, which agreed to give the national government limited powers while retaining most powers for themselves. Jefferson supported a weak national union that performed various narrow functions and allowed the states to go their own ways on other issues.

Indeed, Jefferson and James Madison believed that states had the power to "nullify" laws. When Congress passed the Alien and Sedition Act in 1798, allowing the national government to punish newspaper editors who published stories criticizing the government, the two men penned the Virginia and Kentucky Resolutions. These documents argued that the states voluntarily gave up some sovereignty to join a union, but that they retained the ability to judge the constitutionality of a law and to nullify it if they so desired. The Alien and Sedition Act expired before the Supreme Court could rule on its constitutionality or on the more general question of nullification.

On the other side was Alexander Hamilton, who argued that the national government must be sovereign and that its powers were only vaguely constrained by the Constitution. Hamilton believed that the national government must take the lead in developing the economy of the new nation and in conducting foreign affairs and that only a strong national government could perform these tasks. The struggle between the Jeffersonian and the Hamiltonian visions of the national government has endured throughout US history, with the latter's stronger national government argument ultimately prevailing.

One of the key results of the federal system is the immense power of the judiciary. Because there are inevitably disputes between and among states, as well as between states and the federal government, the federal judiciary is charged often to resolve the disputes. A multilayered system with many governmental entities naturally increases the propensity toward intergovernmental legal conflict.

The Supreme Court has handed down key rulings on the supremacy of the national government's laws, the limits to the government's necessary and proper powers, and the ability of the national government to regulate interstate commerce. These key rulings helped create a more powerful national government than Jefferson had advocated.

Chapter 3

The evolution of federalism in law

Debates over the relative power of the national and state governments have typically hinged on constitutional provisions. Early in US history, some leaders assumed that the national government's powers were limited only to those listed in the Constitution, and thus most uncertainty regarding federal authority hinged on what kinds of laws and programs were "necessary and proper" to carry out the enumerated powers.

The early republic and the nineteenth century

In the early years of the republic, the US Supreme Court played a key role in defining the nature and scope of the US federal system. The case of *Ware v. Hylton* (1796) represents the first instance of judicial nullification of a state law. In a divided opinion, the court ruled that a section of the Treaty of Paris between the United States and Great Britain took precedence over a Virginia statute. This treaty established that British creditors may recover debts from US citizens, in contradiction to a Virginia law that canceled such debts for its citizens. The court established the principle that the treaty power resided exclusively with the federal government and could not be overridden by any state law.

Marbury v. Madison (1803) established the principle of judicial review—the right of the courts to determine the meaning of the law and of the Constitution. From that principle came important court decisions that affirmed the supremacy of the national government. In *Fletcher v. Peck* (1810), the Supreme Court for the first time held a state law to be unconstitutional. The Georgia state legislature had passed a law invalidating a land deal after there were charges of corruption. The court determined that, under the Constitution's contract clause (Article I, Section 10, Clause I), a state law cannot overturn a legally binding contract.

In *Martin v. Hunter's Lessee* (1816), the court overturned a Virginia Supreme Court decision that had upheld a state law allowing Virginia to confiscate the properties of loyalists to the British Crown. Because the state law had conflicted with the terms of a federal treaty, the US Supreme Court declared that a state government and the national government are not coequal sovereigns and that the supremacy clause (Article IV, Clause 2) of the federal Constitution intended that federal interpretations of federal laws and treaties supersede state interpretations.

One early debate was over the establishment of a national bank. Each of the states had chartered its own banks, but federalists such as Alexander Hamilton pushed for a national bank, which he saw as vital to underwriting a national economic system; Thomas Jefferson and his allies opposed it.

The Supreme Court unanimously affirmed in *McCulloch v. Maryland* (1819) that the federal Constitution is the supreme law of the land and that Congress has the right and power to make "all laws . . . necessary and proper" to fulfill its constitutional duties. The court decision emanated from a Maryland state effort to impose a prohibitive tax on the operation of the Second Bank of the United States, chartered by Congress in 1816. Chief Justice Marshall's opinion reasoned that because the Constitution is the supreme law, Maryland could not pass a law that would effectively oppose a right the Constitution had given to Congress, and thus the state law was unconstitutional. Marshall wrote that the power to tax is the power to destroy and that the states did not have the right to destroy a national bank because the national government is supreme. The Marshall court thus affirmed that no state may enact a law to override or contradict the US Constitution. As Marshall saw it, the explicit powers of Congress were *sole province* of the national government, and the necessary and proper clause authorized the Congress to utilize whatever means might be useful for effecting its powers, including establishing a national bank.

This broad interpretation of congressional powers gave Congress much more power than the Constitution had explicitly provided. In place of "necessary," the language in the decision substituted "appropriate" and "not prohibited." As a consequence, the potential powers of the national government were significantly expanded.

In *Cohens v. Virginia* (1821), the Supreme Court affirmed its authority to override the decision of a state supreme court in a criminal matter that violated the constitutional rights of US citizens. The state of Virginia argued in the case that the decision of a state-level supreme court was not reviewable by the federal courts and thus was final. In this case, the state supreme court had rendered an interpretation of a federal law. The US Supreme Court declared that its constitutional grant of jurisdiction (Article III, Section 2, states that the US Supreme Court has jurisdiction in "all Cases, in Law and Equity, arising under this Constitution, the Laws of the United States, and Treaties made, or which shall be made, under their Authority") applied to state courts as well as to cases in which a state is a party and that the supremacy clause renders federal law superior to state law.

The Constitution gave the national government the right to regulate commerce among the states. The commerce clause has been the source of much of the expansion of national government power. From the start, there were disagreements as to the scope of this power, and disagreements remain today. In an important decision that expanded the federal role, the Supreme Court, in *Gibbons v. Ogden* (1824), weighed a conflict between two parties over the use of the Hudson River by steamships. New York gave Aaron Ogden a monopoly on the operation of a steamboat service, and Congress gave Thomas Gibbons a similar license to operate there. Chief Justice Marshall, writing for the court majority, ruled that the New York law was invalid because of the constitutional "supremacy clause" that declares that the federal constitution, federal laws, and federal treaties are the supreme law of the land. Marshall further determined that under the commerce clause, Congress may regulate any interstate commerce as long as it occurs between one state and another, and no individual state has power over it. This case established an important precedent enabling a very broad interpretation of Congress's authority to regulate interstate commerce.

The Supreme Court vastly expanded that federal power in *Wabash, St. Louis and Pacific Railroad v. Illinois* (1886), a decision that led directly to the creation of the nation's first independent regulatory commission, the Interstate Commerce Commission, in 1887. The case arose over controversies regarding the regulation of railways. States had their own regulatory bodies with varied authorities and policies, and rail companies operated under a complex multistate system. In states with little or no regulation, rail companies operated without restriction and abuses were common. There was no system in place for controlling rail rates. The issue was particularly vexing given the vastly increased interstate transport of goods that was critical to the national economy. The court established the ultimate power of the federal government to regulate any and all interstate commerce, which ultimately resulted in the Interstate Commerce Commission having authority to regulate not only railroads, but also all forms of interstate commerce, including trucking, shipping, and oil pipelines.

3. A truck driver logs his hours, in accordance with the Interstate Commerce Act of 1887. After railroads' alleged abuses of economic power, the US Senate designated the Interstate Commerce Commission to regulate the transportation industries.

Throughout much of the nation's first century, the Supreme Court tried to distinguish between business activity that was primarily within a state and that which was done across state lines. Shipping products across state lines was considered interstate commerce, but creating a product in the first place was intrastate commerce and was not subject to national regulation. By the middle of the twentieth century, the United States had largely shifted from an agricultural to an industrial economy, and the court came to recognize the extent to which even the most local economic activity had implications for interstate commerce. Even farmers who grew crops purely for their own consumption, the court said, were subject to Congress's crop quotas.

Nothing in US history tested the unity of the nation nearly so much as the Civil War of 1861–65, when several of the Deep South states seceded and president Abraham Lincoln commanded that federal armies force those states back into the Union. Although the war was largely fought over the institution of slavery, the Southern states claimed that the federal government had no authority to compel any state to remain in the Union and that the war was therefore in large part over states' rights in a federal system. Because the states had given their consent to join a national union in voting to ratify the Constitution, the Southern states thus reasoned that they had the right to withdraw their consent. The victory of the Union Army effectively settled the issue of national unity permanently, although military defeat did not end raging debates over the status of the states in the Union.

The Supreme Court, however, settled the issue as a matter of constitutional law in the case *Texas v. White* (1869), in which the majority ruled that Texas, which became a state in 1850, had permanently joined the Union and thus had remained a legal state even through the period of the Civil War. Thus, all ordinances of secession and acts of state legislatures during the period of secession were null and void. The majority opinion drew on the text of the Articles of Confederation, that the union of the states "be perpetual," and then on the words of the Constitution that it was created "to form a more perfect Union." From these words, the court declared, it is clear that the states had consented to be part of a permanently united country. Thus Texas, and the other states, had "entered into an indissoluble relation. All the obligations of perpetual union, and all the guaranties of republican government in the Union, attached at once to the State. The act which consummated her admission into the Union was something more than a compact; it was the incorporation of a new member into the political body. And it was final."

The twentieth and twenty-first centuries

Judicial decisions of the twentieth century continued the expansion of federal authority, although some key decisions ultimately favored the states. Cases have affirmed, for example, that under the commerce clause, Congress may regulate local

38

commercial activity that has a "close and substantial relationship" to interstate commerce (*National Labor Relations Board v. Jones & Laughlin Steel Corporation*, 1937). Further, Congress has control over the regulation of interstate commerce and, under the provisions of the Fair Labor Standards Act (1938), no state may lower its labor standards to gain a commercial advantage over other states (*United States v. Darby Lumber Co.*, 1941). In the case of *Wickard v. Filburn* (1942) the Supreme Court ruled that Congress may regulate any activity that has a substantial effect on commerce, even when the effect is indirect. This decision vastly expanded Congress's authority under the commerce clause.

Yet some decisions have put restrictions on Congress's authority under the commerce clause. In 1990 Congress enacted the Gun-Free School Zones Act, prohibiting the possession of guns on school grounds anywhere in the country. In *United States v. Lopez* (1995), the Supreme Court overturned the law as unconstitutional on the basis that the commerce clause does not give Congress authority to prohibit gun possession, which is not in itself a form of commercial activity. The federal government had argued that guns in school zones would affect commerce because high crime rates increase insurance costs and fewer people are likely to travel to dangerous areas to transact business. The court majority determined that the government's interpretation of its commerce powers was too broad and would effectively give police powers to the federal government. Possessing a gun illegally, the court ruled, is criminal, not commercial, activity. Importantly, the court rejected the argument that the commerce clause is expansive enough to include indirect commercial consequences of noncommercial activity.

The *United States v. Lopez* decision became the first since the New Deal era limiting Congress's authority under the commerce clause. In 2000, citing *Lopez* as precedent, the Supreme Court in *United States v. Morrison* held portions of the Violence against Women Act of 1994 unconstitutional because Congress had exceeded its authority under the commerce clause. The court determined that the indirect economic effects of violent crimes against women did not present a remedy through the federal government's power to regulate commerce.

These two decisions somewhat reversed earlier rulings that had understood the power to regulate commerce very broadly to include any activity that has economic consequences. By contrast, the court majority in these more recent cases ruled that the commerce clause does not cover activity that is not directly economic in nature, even if it has some economic effects.

The Supreme Court has affirmed the power of the federal government to protect and expand citizen rights when they are violated by state and local policies and actions. The landmark case *Brown v. Board of Education of Topeka, Kansas* (1954) held that no state is permitted to establish racially segregated public schools. The unanimous decision had overturned the odious 1896 Supreme Court decision in *Plessy v. Ferguson* that held that racially segregated, or "separate but equal," public schools were not a violation of the rights of black children. When Arkansas enacted laws with the clear intent to nullify the requirements of the *Brown* decision, the Supreme Court in *Cooper v. Aaron* (1958) ruled that the supremacy clause of the Constitution rendered the previous court decision the supreme law of the land that no state may nullify, because the *Marbury* decision had established the court as the final interpreter of the meaning of the Constitution.

Because states have authority over civil laws and procedures, marriage laws in the United States are not uniform. Nonetheless, the US Supreme Court has affirmed the marriage rights of citizens over discriminatory state policies. For decades, various states had laws that created race-based restrictions on marriage. Virginia's antimiscegenation laws and the Racial Integrity Act of 1924 prohibited marriage between persons classified as white and colored. An interracial married couple, Mildred and Richard

Loving, were arrested in Virginia and given the option of serving a year in prison or leaving the state. They left Virginia but ultimately filed suit in federal court, a case that eventually reached the Supreme Court. In *Loving v. Virginia* (1967), the court invalidated all state policies that prohibited marriage on the basis of race.

Marriage rights expanded dramatically in 2015 when the Supreme Court ruled in a 5–4 decision in *Obergefell v. Hodges* that same-sex couples have the right to marry and that no state may prohibit such marriages. The court in this case held that the due process clause of the Constitution and the equal protection clause of the Fourteenth Amendment guaranteed same-sex couples the same right of marriage as heterosexual couples. Opponents of this view argued that the states have the right to establish different marriage laws and that voters in some states had affirmed their preference for "traditional marriage" through referenda. Before that decision the states had varied laws; thirty-six states had legalized same-sex marriages. The issue became particularly problematic when some of the states opposed to same-sex marriage declared their opposition to recognizing the legal marriages of same-sex couples from other states. The full faith and credit clause of the US Constitution requires states to respect and accept each other's public acts, records, and proceedings, although some states do not recognize legal marriages in other states involving persons considered too young or marriages between close relatives. Federal case law allows for these narrow exceptions to application of the full faith and credit clause.

One of the more controversial exercises of federal power over the states involves the use of fiscal incentives to alter states' behaviors. In 1984, Congress passed a law that threatened states with a reduction in federal transportation funds if they did not raise the legal age for drinking alcohol from eighteen to twenty-one. Congress did not have the authority on its own to force a drinking-age requirement on the states. Congress simply told the states it would withhold some federal funds from any states that did not comply. South Dakota challenged Congress's authority to withhold funds from the state in this fashion, but the Supreme Court ruled in *South Dakota v. Dole* (1987) that Congress had acted constitutionally. The court decision determined that Congress has the right to control its own spending and that the states were still free to maintain their own separate, legal drinking-age laws. Doing so meant losing some federal funds, but Congress had not taken away the states' ultimate authority to make their own decisions. Today, all fifty states and the District of Columbia have a legal drinking age of twenty-one.

Although the national government has many tools to influence state policymaking and to enact federal policy, states retain important powers in the United States. For many Americans, the actions of state and local governments have a bigger impact on their lives than the actions of the national government.

Chapter 4
What state and local governments do

Even as most Americans fix their gaze on the actions of the federal government, states and localities are the cornerstones of the US federal system. With so many state and local government units, it is complicated to present a general framework of their operations. Yet certain general principles do apply.

State government design

States are free to design their own governments so long as their structure does not violate the US Constitution. On rare occasions, the Supreme Court has ruled that the design of a state government does violate the Constitution. In 1964, it ruled in *Reynolds v. Sims* that no state legislative chamber could be apportioned in a manner similar to that of the US Senate—that is, none could have a fixed number of members per county or township. Instead, "one man, one vote" must be the principle in apportioning state legislatures.

All states have designed their state governments to somewhat resemble the national government, with an elected governor, elected legislatures, and state supreme courts. But states are not required to adopt this model—if it chose, a state could have a parliamentary system of government, with a prime minister who is part of the legislature.

Although all states have governors, these executives have very different powers. New York governors can serve as long as voters elect them, and they have other powers that enable them to play a very important role in state politics. In Virginia, the governor may not serve consecutive terms. This means from the first day in office, a governor in Virginia is a lame duck—and state legislators know that they are likely to remain in office long after any particular governor leaves. Most states limit governors to two consecutive terms, but some have higher limits. And in California, Arizona, and some other states, governors are not assured that they will even serve out their term, because voters can recall them in a special election if enough citizens sign a petition. The actor Arnold Schwarzenegger won the California governorship as a Republican in 2003 in a special election after the voters had recalled the incumbent governor, Democrat Gray Davis.

Governors also differ in their formal powers. In some states, governors appoint key officials without consultation, but in other states they need approval by some other body or even lack the power to appoint officials at all. In many states, key state officials are elected, not appointed, and may in fact not be from the governor's party.

In some states, the governor dominates the state budget, whereas in other states, the legislature writes the budget. In some states, a governor's veto is very difficult to override; in others it is far easier. Many states provide governors with a line-item *veto*, which enables them to veto single provisions or even single words in bills—a power that the US Constitution forbids the president to exercise. In a few cases, governors have been able to change the meaning of a bill by vetoing words or phrases such as "not."

Most states have an office of lieutenant governor who, like the US vice president, is first in the line of succession should the chief executive resign, die while in office, or be removed. But five states (Arizona, Maine, New Hampshire, Oregon, and Wyoming) do not have this office. Should the governor of Arizona, Oregon, or Wyoming not complete his or her term, the secretary of state assumes the office for the remainder of the term, and in Maine and New Hampshire, the president of the state senate is next in line to be governor. Upon succession, in most states the new governor assumes the full title, authority, and salary. But in a few states, such as Massachusetts, the title of *acting governor* is conferred until the next election chooses a new governor.

In most states the lieutenant governor is elected as part of a political party ticket along with the governor, just as the United States elects together a president and vice president. But in some states, such as Virginia, there is separate balloting for governor and lieutenant governor. Thus, at times, a member of one political party is elected governor, and the candidate of the opposite party is elected lieutenant governor. In Tennessee and in West Virginia the lieutenant governor is elected by the legislature and serves concurrently as the president of the state senate.

An antiquated provision of the California state constitution, drafted in 1849, dictates that a governor must be within the state's borders at any time to exercise the powers of his office. Thus, when the governor travels out of state, the job of governor transfers to the lieutenant governor until the governor returns. But consider what happens if the lieutenant governor also is out of state. In 2016 there was a most unusual case when governor Jerry Brown, along with the first eight officials in the gubernatorial line of succession, attended the Democratic Party National Convention in Philadelphia, thus leaving the powers of his office to the ninth in succession, the state superintendent of public instruction, who declared upon becoming acting governor, "Don't worry, you're in safe hands."

All states have elected legislatures, and all but Nebraska, which has a unicameral legislature, have two chambers. But state legislatures vary considerably in important ways. Some legislatures have term limits on legislative office, which means that lawmakers must leave office after a set period, usually six years. In 2012, Californians approved a ballot proposition that limits legislators to no more than twelve years of elected service, whether in the state assembly, the state senate, or a combination of both. Most states do not have term limits, so lawmakers can stay in office as long as the voters support them.

More important, nine states have full-time legislatures, where lawmakers meet throughout the year, but six states have legislatures that meet only every other year, and most other states have legislatures that meet for only a few weeks every year. Full-time legislatures are usually professional bodies, with clear rules, significant staff support, and real responsibility. Many part-time legislatures are amateur bodies with little staff, fewer institutionalized rules, and less power. But some part-time legislatures have significant staff who continue to function during off-session periods of time.

Legislative bodies vary greatly in size. New Hampshire has 400 members in its state assembly, California has 80, and Alaska has 40. This means that a state assembly member in New Hampshire represents just 3,000 people and can personally knock on the doors of every family he or she represents, while in the California assembly, members represent about 465,000 individuals—and in the California state senate they represent about 930,000 people. State legislatures differ in their internal rules—in some, power is concentrated in the hands of party leaders, and in others, authority is more decentralized.

All states have supreme courts (not always by that name, however) that interpret the state's constitution. But these justices are chosen differently, and this influences their role in state politics. In West Virginia, justices are elected in partisan elections to twelve-year terms, and in Wisconsin they are elected in nonpartisan elections to ten-year terms. In New York, they are appointed by the governor and approved by the state senate, and in California they are appointed by the governor but then must face the voters five years later in an election to determine whether they remain in office. Additionally, some states have separate final courts of appeal for criminal and for civil cases, and some have both, in addition to a supreme court.

Twenty-six states allow citizens to bypass their state governments and make policy directly by initiative or popular referendum. An initiative allows citizens to propose a new law or constitutional amendment and gather petitions to place it on the ballot. A popular referendum is a citizen proposal to repeal a law previously enacted by the state government. Compared to initiatives, popular referenda are quite rare. Initiatives and popular referenda also are used by thousands of counties, towns, and cities in the United States. There is no national-level provision for such direct citizen action to make or repeal policy.

Most uniquely, each state has its own constitution. Some other countries such as Germany have state constitutions, but they are generally brief and mostly describe the state governments. In the United States, state constitutions also define government institutions and the conduct of elections. But they do much more than this, conferring basic rights on those who live in the states. State constitutions cannot contradict the national constitution, and they cannot limit civil rights conferred to all in the Bill of Rights.

State constitutions can provide stronger protections than the national government for certain rights. For example, the US Constitution states that Congress cannot forbid the free exercise of religion, but it does not say that Congress cannot limit or regulate the free exercise of religion. California's constitution, by contrast, says that "free exercise and enjoyment of religion without discrimination or preference are guaranteed."

Moreover, states can provide additional rights in their constitutions. Privacy is explicitly protected in the California constitution, but it is only implied in the US Constitution. The meaning of California's constitutional privacy right is up to the state's supreme court. One policy that flows from this constitutional provision is that California pays for abortions for poor women. State constitutions vary in their protection of equality. But state constitutional protections of equality have other consequences as well, including the funding of public schools. In many states, public schools are funded by the property tax, which collects more revenues from wealthy communities (with more expensive homes) than from poor communities. This funding mechanism creates vast inequities in educational quality, depending entirely on location. In some states, such as Vermont, the state supreme court has ruled that the revenues raised by the property tax must be distributed more equally across school districts, regardless of the local tax bases.

Local governments are not mentioned in the Constitution, and they have no protected roles. However, in some countries, such as India, the powers and duties of local governments are spelled out in the national constitution. In the United States, state governments can preempt local laws and can deny local governments the right to impose taxes or even limit local tax rates. The preempting of local authority has been especially common in the area of gun control, where cities often want laws regulating the sale of guns, but surrounding rural areas oppose them. In many states, cities are forbidden to limit the sale of guns. Some states have even made it a criminal offense for a city official to sue a gun manufacturer.

State lawmaking

State governments pass laws, regulate private conduct and businesses, and are the principal source of funds for many of the programs that Americans care about most, such as schools, roads, libraries, and municipal services. The national government has the authority to pass criminal laws that generally fall into two broad categories: laws affecting interstate crimes, such as smuggling drugs, trafficking in humans, terrorism, and organized crime; and laws about crimes against the national government, such as threatening the life of the president, killing a federal official, stealing federal secrets, espionage, treason, or failing to pay federal taxes. A majority of prisoners in federal prisons are there for violating drug laws.

But there are limits to federal criminal law. Consider the Unborn Victims of Violence Act, signed into law by president George W. Bush in 2004, which makes the killing of a pregnant woman a double homicide. However, the law applies only to those murders that are under the jurisdiction of the federal government—killing a federal worker while she is on the job, killing a woman on federal property, doing so during the commission of another federal crime such as a drug sale, or killing a member of the national military. There have been few cases that would fall under the law. The principle underlying this federal law appeals to opponents of abortion who believe that a fetus is a person and thus should have the same legal protections as anyone who has been born. Americans' views on this issue vary widely, and thus many socially conservative states have passed similar laws that affect many more situations than the federal statute does.

Most crimes, however, are handled by the states, which provide most of the police, courts, and prisons. Criminal law differs across the states in three ways. First, the penalties for the same crime differ from state to state. Murder is punishable by death in twenty-eight states, but some states use the death penalty far more than others. In some states with death penalty laws, no criminal has been executed in many years. California has the death penalty but has not executed a prisoner since 2006. Today, about one-fourth of all death-row prisoners in the United States are in a

California prison with little likelihood of ever being executed. Texas, by contrast, executes by far the most prisoners of any state: over five hundred since 1976, or about five times the number of executions in Virginia, the state with the second highest number of executions. States can choose the method of execution, and although most states now use lethal injections, some, such as Utah, permit prisoners to choose the firing squad or death by hanging. Widespread shortages of drugs used in lethal injections have slowed the rate of executions in several states, because many companies and countries refuse to provide drugs for this use.

Second, state laws also differ in how they define particular crimes. Possession of less than two ounces of marijuana in Texas is a misdemeanor punishable by a fine of up to $2,000 and a jail term of up to 180 days. Possession of between two and four ounces is a misdemeanor punishable by a fine of up to $4,000 and a sentence of up to one year in jail. Possession of more than an ounce of marijuana is a felony in the state of Georgia and is punishable by up to ten years in prison. In nine states, possession of marijuana is not a crime.

Public drunkenness laws apply in bars in Texas, but only in public places in California. Sexual assault laws differ in their definitions of assault and in the protections they provide for victims in the legal process.

Finally, some actions are legal in some states but illegal in others. Oregon allows physicians to assist in the suicide of a terminally ill patient, but in other states such actions would constitute a felony. Several states allow medical patients to grow their own marijuana, although the national government has the right to prosecute these individuals for violating national drug laws. In nine states it is legal to sell or to purchase and consume marijuana. In the other forty-one states, one can be arrested and/or fined under state law for doing exactly the same thing. In states that have legalized marijuana, the laws vary. In Alaska, for example, it is legal for adults over twenty-one years of age to possess up to one ounce of marijuana for personal use. Alaskans may cultivate up to six marijuana plants for personal use. Gifting and sharing marijuana in small amounts also is legal in the state. In Washington State, adults may possess less than one ounce for private consumption, but the sale or distribution of marijuana is a felony, punishable by up to five years in prison and a $10,000 fine. In Washington, DC, it is legal to possess up to two ounces of marijuana for personal use and to grow up to six plants per person—but not more than twelve in one household—and the sale and distribution of marijuana plants are legal.

States allow local governments to pass criminal laws. In Texas, forty-six counties ban the sale of alcohol completely. Individuals are allowed to possess alcohol in their homes in small amounts, but they cannot buy it in the county. It is legal to drive to a "wet" county and drink in a bar there, but driving home is difficult since the statewide driving-under-the-influence laws apply everywhere.

Prostitution is legal in only one state, Nevada, which allows all counties of fewer than four hundred thousand to license brothels. There are periodic attempts to make prostitution illegal in Nevada, strongly supported by the casino industry, which prefers instead that visitors to Nevada spend their time and money gambling. In all other states, prostitutes and/or their clients can be arrested.

States cooperate in dealing with criminal matters. They are required by the US Constitution to honor extradition requests, so that someone who commits a murder in Texas but is arrested in West Virginia (which does not have the death penalty) will always be sent to Texas to stand trial. States cooperate in the pursuit and arrest of criminals.

The national government cannot require states to spend money in implementing national criminal law. Thus, an Alaska citizen with a small amount of marijuana in his home is subject to federal law, but state and local police are not required to investigate him. The federal government has, at times, implored state and local police to enforce federal immigration policies, but has encountered conflicting state and local policies and even outright opposition. For example, under Maryland law, without a criminal arrest warrant signed by a judge, state law enforcement authorities my not arrest someone they suspect is violating federal immigration laws. Some localities, such as San Francisco and Seattle, have established their status as sanctuary cities—municipalities that limit or even oppose cooperation with federal efforts to enforce immigration laws.

Civil law differs across states as well. Civil law covers contracts, including marriage and divorce and efforts to recover damages from individuals and companies who have harmed someone. States have different laws regulating families, including marriage, divorce, and child custody. Some states (Arizona, Arkansas, and Louisiana) allow couples to choose between a regular marriage and a covenant marriage. Regular marriages can end in a no-fault divorce after a six-month separation, but divorce is far more difficult in a covenant marriage. Couples who enter into this type of marriage contract are required to seek marriage counseling before divorce, and the contract can be ended only for a limited number of reasons, such as adultery, commission of a felony by a spouse, or spousal or child abuse. Before entering into this kind of marriage, the couple must certify that they intend to remain married forever, that they have undergone premarital counseling, and that they have fully informed each other of all issues that might affect the marriage.

For regular marriage, some states require a waiting period between application and receipt of a marriage license. In Nevada, however, there is no such waiting period, and in Las Vegas it is even possible to marry without leaving your car. Also,

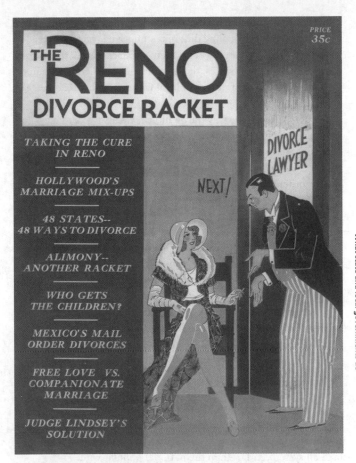

4. Divorce lawyers in the 1920s helped their clients establish temporary residency in Nevada, one of the only states where divorce was universally legalized at the time. In the United States, individual states have the authority to regulate marriage and divorce.

uncontested divorces are relatively easy to obtain in Nevada—so much so that some citizens of other states fly to Nevada and establish residence by staying there for six weeks so that they can divorce more easily.

Marriage and divorce contracts made in any state are honored by other states. But reconciling different state civil laws is not easy. If a couple marries in one state and then, once separated, the parties move to two different states, there is only one predictable result— they will spend a lot of money in legal fees if they divorce.

States also differ in the way they handle lawsuits for damages. For example, imagine that you are in a car accident that is mostly the other driver's fault, but you could possibly have avoided the accident if you had reacted more quickly. In some states, you could sue the other driver for full damages, in others you could sue the driver for only a percentage of your damages because you are partially to blame, and in still other states you could not sue at all.

Differences in state laws regarding lawsuits against doctors have created unequal costs for malpractice insurance across the country. In some cases, doctors may even relocate in a neighboring state to lower their costs. Texas, for example, has seen a large influx of new doctors since its 2003 enactment of malpractice reforms that limited physician liability, resulting in fewer lawsuits and lower insurance rates for doctors.

Conducting elections

The United States does not have a national election system; instead, elections are conducted by the states. For the presidency, candidates in the general election run to win states, in a winner-take-all system, rather than the national popular vote. The Electoral College in the case of forty-eight states and the District of Columbia awards 100 percent of the electors to the winner of the vote within each state (and the District of Columbia). Two states, Maine and Nebraska, distribute their electoral votes on a different basis: the winner of the popular vote in each House of Representatives district is awarded one elector, and the winner of the state popular vote is awarded two at-large electors. States have the discretion to adopt their own systems of distributing electors, but right now the winner-take-all system dominates. On five occasions, the winner of the national popular vote lost the election in the Electoral College. The most recent cases are Donald J. Trump, who won merely 46 percent of the popular vote in 2016 but a narrow majority of the electors to the Electoral College, and George W. Bush, who in 2000 won the Electoral College after a long, disputed vote count in the state of Florida.

The Electoral College is an important feature of the federal system in that it ensures that general election candidates do not merely center their election quests on large population centers and states. Small states matter, and therefore candidates must appeal to both urban and rural interests and run broad-based national campaigns rather than regional ones. That is the only way to achieve a majority of electors. Small state delegates at the Constitutional Convention objected to a national popular election system on the basis that the interests of smaller states would be overlooked in national elections. The Electoral College was a compromise forged at the convention after numerous alternative means of picking presidents had been rejected.

The outcome of the presidential election of 2000 rested in part on a federalism dispute. With the vote count in Florida too close to call definitively and the outcome of the election hinging on that one state, the state of Florida had to recount the ballots, many of which were in dispute because of old voting technology that used perforated punch cards. On some of the punch cards, voter intent was not clear, and elections officials, lawyers, and campaign officials battled over the counts for over a month after Election Day. Given the uncertainty of the recount and allegations of voting irregularities as well, the supreme court of Florida had ordered that the counting of the ballots continue. The George W. Bush campaign filed a federal suit that became the basis for the US Supreme Court decision in *Bush v. Gore* (2000), in which the court majority by a vote of 5–4 mandated the end of the recount, at which point Bush was in the lead and thereby elected president.

Substantial controversy ensued in legal circles and beyond as to the correctness of the court's reasoning given that the state of Florida had jurisdiction over the conduct of its own state election and the state supreme court was the ultimate authority on state law and procedures. Questions of state law traditionally are left to state courts, but in this case the US Supreme Court declared that a compelling national interest in settling the election was overriding. Critics of the court decision were quick to point out the irony that the conservative majority generally had been deferential to the states in other federalism disputes.

Local governments

States are divided into a form of governing subunits called counties, which are an outgrowth of the colonial era of US history. Counties vary substantially in size and governing functions. There are more than three thousand counties in the United States. Some are larger than the populations of states—Los Angeles County, for example, has more than ten million residents. Yet some counties are merely several thousand people. Delaware has only 3 counties, whereas Texas has 254. Counties are usually governed by elected bodies that use titles such as board of supervisors or county commission.

Within counties, typically there are independently incorporated municipalities, although New York City uniquely is partitioned into multiple counties called *boroughs*. There is also the designation of a *county equivalent*, which is an administrative territory that has legal functions and duties similar to those of a county. Examples are the Louisiana parishes and the District of Columbia, and within several states there are independent cities that do not exist within any county territory (e.g., Baltimore, Maryland, and St. Louis, Missouri).

Cities and townships may be separately incorporated as local governments and thus have their own elected officials and local laws and regulations. Some states require that cities and townships exist within the territory of a single county, whereas other states allow such local units to extend across the boundaries of counties.

County, city, town, and village governments do a lot, but they have no constitutional status in the United States, and they are legally the creations of the states. Therefore, state constitutions and laws determine the allowable authority and fiscal operations of local governments. Some states operate with what is known as the Dillon rule—derived from two court decisions issued in 1868 by judge John F. Dillon of Iowa and upheld by the US Supreme Court in 1907—which is that localities only possess those powers that have been specifically granted to them by the state legislature. In contrast, in home-rule states, local governments have discretion to make a wide range of policy decisions without direction by the state. The benefits of the Dillon rule are that it constrains local governments from operating irresponsibly and putting burdens on the rest of the state, and it ensures some degree of policy uniformity throughout the state. Advocates of home rule counter that the spirit of federalism in the United States is to allow as much local discretion as possible to enable communities to solve problems in different ways and not be subject to the decisions of the state.

Among the responsibilities and services of local governments are zoning law, traffic control, sanitation collection, street repair, educational administration, public parks and libraries, recreation centers, administration of courts and jails, and public health services, among others. Local governments provide different menus and levels of these services.

In Fairfax County, Virginia, for example, the county government for years provided for sanitation and recycling collection using a single service provider that had a contract with the government. The elected county board then decided to eliminate this public service, thus requiring homeowners to hire private contractors to provide it. Townships and cities within the country have varied policies, making it common for homeowners who live close to each other but in different jurisdictions to have vastly different public services. Philosophical and practical debates have raged over what the government's responsibility is to provide for such services, as opposed to relying on a free market of service providers, and ultimately what is the most efficient and effective way to collect refuse and recycled goods. A federal structure allows for this kind of variation in policies.

Native American reservations

The unique legal status of Native American lands goes back to the Constitution itself. Article 1, Section 8, reads, in part, "to regulate Commerce with foreign Nations, and among the several States, and with the Indian Tribes." The founders thus understood the Native American lands as neither states nor foreign nations. The US government, and not the states, thus made treaties with the Indian tribes.

Today, federally recognized tribes manage Native American reservations and other tribal lands under the authority of the US Bureau of Indian Affairs. The *tribal nations* are recognized under US law as domestic, dependent nations and they have an inherent right to govern themselves, although the Indian lands are held in trust by the federal government. But the US government and federal laws still regulate much of their political and economic activity.

Tribes lack jurisdiction over non-Indians who are accused of crimes on Indian lands. Otherwise, they can make and enforce their own laws, both civil and criminal, impose taxes, license and regulate commercial and other activity in their jurisdictions, and exercise zoning authority. Some tribes have their own constitutions, and most operate their governments with a system of separation of powers (legislative, executive, and judicial).

The relationship between the states and Indian tribes is somewhat complicated. States would prefer to have authority within their jurisdictions to regulate the activities of Indian tribes, but federal court decisions have ruled that past treaties with the Indian nations, acts of Congress, executive orders, and executive agreements are the controlling authority. These issues come into conflict, for example, when Indian tribes engage in such commercial enterprises as gaming and the states want to have regulatory control.

US territories

There are five permanently inhabited US territories: Puerto Rico, the US Virgin Islands, Guam, the Northern Mariana Islands, and American Samoa. Each became a territory in a different manner. Puerto Rico, for example, was a Spanish colony until in 1898, when the United States gained control of it in the agreement that ended the Spanish–American War. Puerto Rico existed as an unincorporated territory until a federal law in 1917 granted Puerto Ricans US citizenship. In 1948, the US government approved a constitution of Puerto Rico and established it as a commonwealth. Territories of the United States may apply for statehood status. In June 2017, the citizens of Puerto Rico voted in favor of statehood in a popular referendum. However, this referendum is nonbinding, because only Congress can approve statehood for a territory.

With the exception of American Samoa, inhabitants of the territories are US citizens. Under the Immigration and Nationality Act, American Samoa's residents are considered nationals and may apply to become naturalized citizens. Each of the territories has its own elected system of government and has a delegate (or *resident commissioner*, in the case of Puerto Rico) in the US

Congress who may vote in committee but not in the full House of Representatives. All of the territories, except American Samoa, have a system for appealing cases to the US federal district courts. American Samoa's final court is the Samoan High Court. The US secretary of the interior appoints American Samoa's chief justice, and the territorial governor appoints the lower judges. In the remaining four territories, the elected governor appoints the judges. The two major political parties assign delegate slots at their national nominating conventions every four years to the five US territories. But the citizens of the territories cannot vote in the general election.

The US federal system's vast array of state, local, and territorial governments can be confusing to those unfamiliar with the country's traditions and practices. Indeed, understanding the system is complicated even for US citizens themselves. In practice, US government policies demonstrate that the needs of the territories are a relatively low priority. In 2017, for instance, a massive hurricane devastated the island of Puerto Rico, leaving as many as 80 percent of the people without electricity for weeks and even months. The federal response was slow and highly inadequate, in marked contrast to the federal response to another massive hurricane a month earlier that caused severe damage in Houston, Texas. Advocates of statehood status for Puerto Rico picked up support after the hurricanes, in part as a result of the perception that US federal policies would better serve the island under state, rather than territorial, status. The governor of Puerto Rico even pleaded with President Trump to put an end to the United States' "territorial-colonialism" and support statehood, but the president refused.

Chapter 5
Fiscal federalism

During the early decades of the republic, Congress gave the states money to help pay for new roads and canals and to help them support their militias. The national government also gave funds to the states to build colleges and universities. Some of the founders, including James Madison, believed that these federal grants exceeded the national government's constitutional powers. But over time, the view that the national government could give states money to help them achieve a shared goal became widespread. During the 1860s, the national government made land grants to the states to set up new colleges and universities to teach agriculture, mining, industry, and military tactics. Many of these large, land-grant universities are among the finest universities in the United States today, including the University of California at Berkeley, Cornell University, and the University of Wisconsin at Madison.

But the system of granting money to the states came into its own in the twentieth century, especially after the Sixteenth Amendment gave the national government the right to impose an income tax in 1913, which greatly enhanced the national government's revenue. During the twentieth century, the total amount that the national government gave to the states, and the range of programs for which this money was given, exploded. It continues to grow.

Federal grants

Early in the twentieth century, federal grant programs totaled only a few million dollars. Total federal aid to state and local governments in fiscal year 2019 was $749 billion. There are more than 1,100 federal aid programs today, each with its own set of rules and regulations.

This drastic change greatly increased the power of the federal government to influence policies that are not among the list of enumerated powers in the Constitution. But federal grants may also provide some added flexibility to the states. Federal grants have the effect of somewhat reducing federal bureaucracy by allowing states to carry out some federal policies. Different states often have different approaches to solving similar policy problems, and some federal grants recognize this need and allow for state flexibility. In short, what works in Texas may not work so well in New York, but each state can reach toward achieving a common federal goal in the manner that best suits its own situation.

Federal grants also have the benefit of somewhat reducing the maldistribution of resources among the states. Consider public education, which is primarily funded by state and local taxes, especially the annual personal property tax on the value of citizens' land and homes. Wealthier communities with higher local tax revenues generally have the best public schools in the United States. The disparity in educational resources and thus quality of education is staggering in the United States. Nonetheless, federal aid programs directed toward lower-income school systems can provide some needed relief where local and state resources are not adequate to meet critical needs. Head Start is one such federal program: it began in 1965 as a summer school program for children in low-income families to receive additional instruction before beginning elementary school, and it developed over time into a more comprehensive early childhood education, health, and nutrition program.

Today, federal grants account for about 30 percent of the average operating revenue of state and local governments. Thus, the subnational government units are heavily dependent on the federal government for funding their own operations. Many of the states also have constitutional requirements to maintain a biannual balanced budget, meaning that they are further restricted in their fiscal flexibility and even more reliant on federal revenues than they would be otherwise, especially during periods of slow economic growth and shrinking tax rolls at the state level. Nonetheless, the federal government has saved states from making drastic cuts in programs during economic downturns by providing substantial relief to the state budgets.

Federal grants therefore provide the national government with a way to induce states to do those things that it cannot force them to do. The national government has no real command power in the field of education, for example. States are not even required by the national constitution to provide public education, and they are certainly not required to teach science or geography. But there is a national Department of Education, and this agency provides funds to the states to accomplish national educational goals. State and local governments can apply for funds from many national educational programs, including programs to aid in the teaching of individuals with special needs and abilities, to aid in the teaching of Native Americans, to provide funds to schools with many poor students, and to teach specific curricula.

The national government gives money to states to do many important things—to provide food, income, and healthcare to the poor; to repair and build new roads and bridges; to train police and build prisons; to help cities provide sewage treatment; and for many other purposes. After the terrorist attacks of September 11, 2001, Congress also gave money to states and cities to help their police and fire departments prepare for emergencies. In 2004, the Savannah, Georgia, fire department received $54,000 in federal funds from the Department of Homeland Security—more than two hundred years after the city had suffered a devastating fire for which it received no federal assistance—to help it buy personal protective equipment for its firefighters.

States can refuse to accept grants from the national government if they do not wish to implement a program or to abide by the guidelines that the program imposes. Until 1982, Arizona refused federal funds for Medicaid, the program that provides healthcare for poor citizens, because the program had required shared costs between the federal government and any participating state. Maine and California have refused money to implement abstinence-only sex education programs in public schools. Some states refuse to accept public funds for public libraries, because taking the money obliges them to install content filters on public computer terminals.

States have come to depend on federal grants, and this gives the national government some leverage to threaten to withhold grants unless the state does various other things. For example, states rely on federal funds to help repair roads, highways, and bridges. To achieve fuel efficiency during a national energy crisis in 1973, Congress passed a law intended to create a nationalized highway speed limit of fifty-five miles per hour by declaring that states either must adopt this requirement or lose federal highway funds. All of the states complied, because the loss of federal highway funds would have had major negative impacts on state budgets. Yet noncompliance with the highway speed limit was extraordinarily high, and in 1995 Congress repealed this enactment; ever since, the states have been able to set their own speed limits.

In the mid-1980s, Congress wanted all states to increase the legal drinking age from eighteen to twenty-one, but the Constitution (in the Twenty-First Amendment) gives states the power to regulate alcohol. Instead, Congress passed a bill that threatened any state that did not increase its drinking age to twenty-one with the loss of some federal highway funds. In a constitutional challenge to this action, the Supreme Court affirmed Congress's right to attach conditions to its grants to the states.

In the early 2000s, during the George W. Bush administration, the US Department of Education issued an incentive to the states to adopt national educational achievement standards in return for federal monies. The states had the discretion to refuse the federal money, but very few did. States that accepted the federal money were thus required to implement the use of periodic standardized examinations, which many educators decried as being formulaic and encouraging "teaching to the test." Although some proponents of the ideals of federalism perceive such an action by the federal government as an intrusion on the powers of the states, the federal response is that the states are not obligated to adopt the federal standards. The states can simply turn down the federal funds and continue to rely on state and local revenue sources to meet their educational needs. Turning down federal money, however, is politically very difficult for the states. Without federal funds, elected official may have to turn to unpopular tactics such as raising state taxes.

Most federal grants are categorical grants—that is, the federal government appropriates funding to states for specific purposes directed by Congress. Medicaid and Head Start are examples of categorical grant programs. States can apply for the money, but if they get it they must use it in narrowly defined ways. Moreover, frequently states must provide matching funds to qualify for federal grants.

Another type of federal grant is the block grant, which is appropriated money for broad programs with few congressional conditions attached. Unlike categorical grants, with a block grant a state has broad discretion regarding how to spend the funding. The most notable example is the program Temporary Assistance for Needy Families. Enacted in 1997, the program provides grants to states to run their own welfare programs. It imposes only very general guidelines for the use of the federal funds, such as providing support for needy families with children at home and promoting job preparation so that recipients do not remain on public assistance for too long.

Additionally, there are project grants, which are monies allocated to states, local governments, and even nongovernmental units after the submission of a competitive application for funding. An example is the Department of Education program enacted in 2009, Race to the Top, which offers competitive grants to states that demonstrate the highest ability to improve educational standards and performance through innovative reforms. Because the grants can be substantial, some states have made changes in their education policies to better meet the criteria in the application process.

In the 1960s and early 1970s, the national government provided general funds to the states in a program of general *revenue sharing*. Although this program no longer exists, there still are limited revenue-sharing grants in particular policy areas, such as education. The revenue-sharing idea was the hallmark of what president Richard M. Nixon had touted as "the new federalism"—a shifting of more federal funding to the states, providing them with discretion in the use of those funds, rather than relying on the national government to direct the use of all of its revenues. Whereas block grants gave discretion to states for spending within program areas, revenue sharing merely shifted funds from the federal government to the states, allowing the states to choose which programs to fund with those revenues.

Federal mandates

The national government has also used mandates to influence state policymaking. When the national government sets standards for clean water or clean air, for example, it does not always provide funding to the states to help them comply with those standards. The costs of compliance with these standards are sometimes quite high—in some cases, cities faced costs of billions of dollars to comply. A good example is the Clean Air Act amendments of 1970 and 1990. These congressional enactments established automotive emissions standards and placed the burden on the states to provide plans to the federal government to implement the standards and fund the costs of implementation.

Congress does not have the power to compel the states to carry out its programs, as Congress learned in 1997 when the Supreme Court struck down the provision of the Brady Handgun Violence Prevention Act law that required state and local law enforcement to conduct criminal background checks on would-be gun buyers.

Instead, the national government has usually enforced these mandates with threats to withhold federal funds from related projects and in some cases has used threats of civil or even criminal sanctions. In 1995, Congress passed a law forbidding the implementation of new unfunded mandates without a debate on how to fund them. Since then, Congress has created new mandates, but at a slower pace. One example is the 2002 No Child Left Behind law, which imposes educational testing requirements on participating states as a condition for receiving any federal funds from the program.

Regulatory law

The national government has the right to regulate interstate commerce, but states retain the right to regulate businesses within their borders. States are also responsible for business and professional licensing. National regulations establish the minimum standards that states generally cannot avoid, but states frequently go beyond those standards to set tougher regulations. For example, the national government has set minimum pollution standards for automobiles, but California has set stricter standards, and several other states have adopted the California standards. Indeed, some automotive manufacturers have adopted the California standard for the entire US market given the cost and complexity of having to otherwise make the same automobile according to multiple standards in the United States. The only workable default position for a single standard is the strictest one in this case—made all the more likely because California is home to about one-seventh of the entire US population. Thus, an interesting feature of US federalism is that states, particularly a very large one such as California or a collection of them, can sometimes effectively drive national policy.

When the George W. Bush administration decided in 2001 not to adopt the Kyoto Protocol on global warming, some state and local governments adopted strict environmental regulations aimed at meeting the standards of that convention. In 2017, when president Donald J. Trump declared that the United States was withdrawing from the Paris Agreement, twenty states and more than fifty cities signed pledges to abide by the environmental standards of the agreement.

States regulate business beyond the national minimum in many other ways. Some states have implemented workplace safety standards aimed at preventing repetitive stress injuries from constant use of computers. Some limit the alcohol content of beer to 3.2 percent, while others prohibit the sale of certain products that violate the state's consumer protection laws.

Health insurance is heavily regulated by states, and laws differ across the country. Nonetheless, the federal government sets the basic guidelines for essential benefits in areas such as emergency, pediatric, and maternity care. There are also federal protections: for example, no state may charge more for insurance coverage based on one's health or gender. However, states can set up their own insurance marketplaces and choose insurance companies, as well as provide more coverage than is required by federal guidelines. Some states allow unlimited competition in the health insurance marketplace, whereas others limit the number of companies that may sell in their markets. Beyond the required federal categories of coverage, states have substantial discretion. For example, some states require insurers to cover weight-loss surgery, whereas others do not.

In many states, all employers must offer at least one healthcare plan that pays the costs of contraception, even if the employer's personal religious views state that contraception is sinful. States also regulate the cost of health insurance, and in some states these regulations have led some insurers to withdraw from the state market.

State budgets and revenues

Although states receive important funds from the national government, they also raise and spend their own funds. States vary in the types of taxes they adopt. Most states tax income, in some cases using the same forms as the federal government. But seven states have no income tax, and two others tax income only from dividends and interest. And state income tax rates vary widely; the highest bracket in Vermont is 9.5 percent of taxable income, but in Illinois it is 3 percent. The structure of income taxes varies as well: in Maryland there is a somewhat progressive tax system, with higher income earners paying more. The highest marginal rate is 5.75 percent, but Maryland counties and the city of Baltimore may impose additional income taxes ranging from 1.75 to 3.2 percent; that additional amount is collected by the state on the annual state income tax form but is returned quarterly to the local governments. The local governments themselves set the rate, within the parameters allowed by the state.

Most states have sales taxes, but five states do not, and states vary in the rate of the tax and whether they exempt sales of food, medicine, and other items. Alaska alone has neither a sales nor an income tax, because its revenue depends primarily on the sale of oil from state-owned lands. But some local governments in Alaska have their own sales taxes. Alaska refunds some of its excess revenue from oil to its residents, making it the only state that not only has no income tax, but also effectively pays people to live there.

Most states also levy taxes on the value of personal property, including houses, automobiles, and boats. Property taxes are often collected by county governments and earmarked for key services such as schools, roads, and police. In areas where property values are increasing sharply, many homeowners face rapidly escalating property taxes—an especially acute problem for senior citizens on fixed incomes who bought their homes years prior, when home values were low. As a result, some states and counties provide special relief on property taxes for senior citizens. Also, some states have passed popular initiatives that impose limits on real estate property tax increases. Most famous is California's Proposition 13, passed in 1978, which reverted rates to 1976 levels and prohibited the state from increasing assessments of property values more than 2 percent in one year.

States also rely on the excise tax—a special tax imposed on the purchases of tobacco, gasoline, and alcohol. Excise-tax rates also vary significantly. Virginia, a traditional tobacco-growing state that depends on the crop as a key source of revenue, has the nation's lowest excise tax on the sale of tobacco. In Virginia, a pack of cigarettes has a state excise tax of $0.30, whereas in neighboring Maryland and the District of Columbia the tax is $2.00 and $2.90, respectively. In New York, the excise tax on cigarettes is a staggering $4.35 per pack—nearly fifteen times the Virginia tax rate. Not surprisingly, it is common for residents of neighboring states to cross state boundaries to buy cheaper products given these substantial differences.

Increasingly, states are relying on gambling to finance public programs. A majority of states now run lotteries. In more than half of these states, the profits are earmarked for public schools, and in Georgia and Florida, for example, the lottery funds go to specific programs, such as college scholarships. Other states have recently allowed slot machines, video poker machines, and riverboat or racetrack gambling, and in each case the state receives licensing fees and often levies a special tax on winnings.

Many groups, both liberal and conservative, argue that gambling is a poor way to pay for government, since it collects money disproportionately from less affluent individuals, who may be enticed to gamble in the hopes of solving financial problems, but in doing so may make those problems worse. Yet the attraction of gambling as a revenue source is clear. When states raise taxes, taxpayers complain. When they create a program of legalized gambling, gamblers are eager to participate, although some of their family members may complain.

Further, gambling revenue may look less attractive when it is used to replace other sources of public spending by the state rather than to supplement state funding. Florida touts that since it instituted the lottery in 1986, the state has contributed more than $30 billion to education. Critics have alleged that this money merely has replaced state funds rather than supplemented them and that overall public spending on education in Florida has not increased much.

Because state tax rates vary, as does the amount of wealth and income available to be taxed, some state governments have much more money than others. Although federal grants help somewhat in alleviating some of the inevitable inequities in the financial capacities of the states, that revenue is not nearly enough to make up the real differences, which can be substantial. The problem is compounded by some states that choose to have very low tax rates and thus provide little support for social safety net programs, education, and other needs. That choice creates a dilemma, because some federal government programs target needy populations, and thus national resources are being redistributed in part to provide revenues that certain states are unwilling to commit on their own.

Spending on state programs

States provide basic services that citizens depend on, and the quality of those services differs from state to state. States with more money can pay more for schools, more for police salaries and equipment, and more for library books and healthcare for poor citizens. Although the national government provides some funding in each of these policy areas, state and local spending is very important in each case. The national government provides only about 10 percent of the funds for public schools, on average, meaning that state and local governments provide the other 90 percent.

The differences in spending between states can be dramatic. New Jersey and New York traditionally spend more than twice as much per pupil in public schools as do Mississippi and Arizona. In 2014, New York spent more than sixty-two dollars per capita for public libraries, whereas Mississippi spent around sixteen dollars. Cost differences between those two states are not insignificant, but do not come close to accounting for this nearly four-to-one ratio. Rich states are able to pave their roads more often, have more books and computers in public libraries, more fully subsidize tuition for state universities and provide more scholarships, and provide better healthcare to the poor than poor states can.

States determine their own school curricula. Kansas has removed the theory of evolution from its statewide science testing. Teachers are still permitted to mention the theory of evolution in teaching biology classes, but since most teachers focus on preparing their students to pass statewide tests, the new policy guarantees that evolution will not be central to the Kansas biology curriculum. However, Kansas had once before removed evolution from its tests, and in response, the voters removed the school board in the next election. Consequently, battles over school curricula in Kansas and elsewhere often become battles at the ballot box.

Public universities are partially funded by the states, because there is no national university system in the United States as there is, for example, in France. Under increasingly constrained budgetary environments since the 1990s, many states have reduced substantially their funding for higher education. Some public colleges and universities have frozen compensation for employees for years and even furloughed faculty for periods of time, cut spending on classroom needs and other academic resources, and raised tuition, although states may also restrict tuition increases. While many public institutions of higher learning have had to adjust to the challenging fiscal environment, some prestigious public universities with large endowments have debated whether they could do better by going private and not having to be regulated by their states and thus eliminate many of the regulatory requirements that states impose on public institutions.

With these differences that exist across states and localities, many political observers reasonably question whether the federal system is the best way to run a nation-state. It is therefore necessary to evaluate how well the federal system operates in comparison to other forms of government.

Chapter 6
Advantages and disadvantages of federalism

The US federal system has advantages and disadvantages over a unitary system and over other types of federal systems. As much as the federal system is the preferred option of Americans, who historically have had a skeptical view of centralized power, not many would say it is perfect system or even that it comes close. Despite its many virtues, shortcomings inherent in the US federal system lead many observers to question whether it is adequate to meet the needs of increasingly complex social and economic problems.

Advantage 1: Flexibility of standards

The United States is a very large and diverse nation, and it is difficult to set regulatory standards that apply equally everywhere. By setting minimum national standards and allowing states to go beyond them, the country can be flexible. Los Angeles needs a stricter air pollution standard than does Fairmont, West Virginia, so West Virginia abides by the national minimum standard environmental protection, while California has adopted a stricter air pollution standard to deal with the air in Los Angeles and other cities.

Of course, flexibility does not mean that states always use that flexibility to deal with problems. The air in Houston is badly polluted too, but Texas has not adopted stricter air pollution standards than the national ones. However, the fact that Houston *can* adopt such standards if its elected officials so choose is an advantage over setting either a single high or a single low standard nationwide.

Advantage 2: Flexibility in dealing with religious diversity

The United States is a religious, and very religiously diverse, nation. Surveys show that about one-third of Americans attend church weekly, and many more go a few times a month. But Americans attend a dazzling array of churches, synagogues, mosques, temples, and other houses of worship. And all these religious bodies teach somewhat different things about morality and law.

The intersection of religion and politics in the United States is less contentious than in Nigeria or India, where large religious communities (Christians and Muslims in Nigeria, Hindus and Muslims in India) have substantial and intense disagreements about law and morality. But it is far more contentious than in Europe, where most countries have established churches but few people are deeply religious.

Federalism provides some flexibility to help avoid religious-based conflict by allowing state and local governments some discretion in dealing with moral issues. Baptist churches mostly teach that the death penalty is God's will, and majority Baptist states such as Texas have the death penalty and use it often. The Catholic Church teaches that only God should take life, and for the most part, states with very large Catholic populations (New York, New Jersey, Rhode Island, Connecticut, Massachusetts) either do not have the death penalty or rarely use it.

Utah has a very large Mormon (Church of Latter-Day Saints) population—more than half the state's residents are adherents. Mormons have a strict moral code—no alcohol, tobacco, or even caffeine is permitted. Hence, Utah is not likely to legalize marijuana.

States differ in their restrictions on abortion: some require parental notification for minors seeking abortions and limit access to health clinics that perform abortions, whereas others have no such restrictions on minors and provide easy access to health clinics. State laws vary significantly with regard to regulating alcohol. They have different laws on marriage and divorce and different policies on teaching sex education. Federalism thus allows Americans to finesse religious differences on moral issues by allowing some states to regulate certain areas of social and moral conduct.

However, the Constitution limits how states can legislate morality. Existing Supreme Court precedents say that states cannot ban homosexual activity by consenting adults in the privacy of their homes and that they cannot prevent adult women from having an abortion in the first six months of their pregnancies if they can find a provider who will perform the procedure. If the Supreme Court overturns the *Roe v. Wade* (1973) decision that legalized abortion, then states would be free to limit abortion as they wished.

Advantage 3: Experimentation

In unitary systems, national governments adopt new policies, and if they fail, they try something new. In the United States and in some other federal systems, not only the federal government but also states and localities experiment with new policies, and if the policies succeed, they are often copied. When California adopted a higher standard for air pollution from automobiles, car manufacturers objected that they would be unable to meet the standard or that it would be prohibitively expensive to do so. Once it became evident that California's standard was technologically feasible, however, several other states copied that standard. Automobile manufacturers adapted to the reality.

States are often called laboratories of experimentation, for good reason. States are always trying new programs in education, healthcare, crime control, and economic growth, and those policies that work quickly spread to other states. For example, in 2012, the states of Colorado and Washington passed laws legalizing marijuana; after observing the outcomes of this new policy, several other states did the same. It is possible that over time, the experiment begun in two states will become policy in most states. In some cases, a successful state policy becomes the model for a future federal program. The successful healthcare reform of Massachusetts in 2006, which provided health insurance to nearly all Massachusetts residents, became the model for the national Affordable Care Act of 2010. States also learn what does not work well and avoid the mistakes of others.

Advantage 4: Policies vary at different levels of government

In a centralized governmental system, failure to achieve policy preferences at the national level is devastating to many, given that there is no option for citizens to pursue alternative polices at the subnational levels in the United States. Failure at the national level inspires many groups and citizens to take their policy battles to the states and to local governments. Some take their challenges to the courts as well. A federal system provides multiple avenues of access for groups and citizens to influence the policy process.

When the US Supreme Court declared abortion a privacy right of all women, socially conservative groups and activists did not give up; rather, they stepped up their efforts to influence state-level policies throughout the country. Since abortion rights became a constitutional guarantee, religious conservatives have lobbied successfully in several states to enact a number of restrictive policies. These include prohibiting the use of taxpayer funds for abortion-related health services; putting expensive and onerous regulations on the operations of medical practices that perform abortions, forcing many to close their businesses; and enacting parental notification and parental consent laws to limit abortions for minors. These groups have also aggressively sought to influence judicial appointments at the state and federal levels to try to further weaken abortion access in the country.

When the national government has not put high priority on environmental protection, numerous states and localities have banded together to effect laws that provide for environmental protections in their areas. Proenvironmental groups and activists have seen that state by state, city by city, they can effect a change in policy that perhaps does not add up fully to a nationalized approach, but comes much closer than if the governmental subunits merely stayed on the sidelines while the national government controlled policy.

Advantage 5: Keeping central government power in check

A federal system ensures that the national government does not become too powerful and that there exists a good deal of local and state-level autonomy in such areas as civil law, criminal law, and public education. Americans customarily have been very suspicious of centralized power, and a federal system enables citizens to have more input in the making of policy where they actually live. "Keep government close to the people" has long been the rallying cry of those who favor a federal system with substantial state and local autonomy and minimal national interference.

Although proponents of centralized power equate a stronger national government with greater governmental efficiency, there is a certain efficiency achieved by allowing policy to match preferences of citizens in their own communities. Further, decentralized government authority encourages citizen participation in public life, because people are more likely to become directly involved in matters affecting their communities than they are to try to effect national political action that is entirely too distant from them. Much research attests to the benefits to a democratic republic of having direct citizen involvement in school boards, library boards, homeowner associations, town councils, city and county governments, and state government. With such involvement, citizens are more likely to understand government institutions and their operations and benefit from the gratification of being a part of the system and making a difference in their communities. Public support for the legitimacy of governmental institutions and policy decisions is enhanced when citizens perceive that they have a direct role.

Advantage 6: Citizen choice

A federal system, particularly in such a large and diverse country as the United States, provides a vast menu of lifestyle choices for its citizens, who can choose where to live based in part on the policies advanced by state and local governments and the predominant values that exist in communities.

Many senior citizens in retirement choose to live in low-tax states such as Florida to better preserve their fixed incomes. Many families with young children choose to live in Maryland, one of the five highest tax states in the United States, primarily because the public school system is ranked among the best in the country. Americans willingly live in a higher-tax state if they believe that the public benefits provided are worth the cost, but then they may retire to one of America's seven states with no income tax.

Values drive many peoples' decisions about where to live. Demographers report that increasingly Americans are sorting themselves into communities of like-minded people, a phenomenon that reflects one of the main virtues of decentralized government—its ability to promote laws that are consistent with peoples' values. Mormons make up about 1 to 2 percent of the US national population, but of Utah's three million residents, about 63 percent are Mormon. Utah's laws very much reflect the belief systems of the majority population there, which tend to be socially very conservative. Yet a person only has to travel a short distance, to Nevada, for a very different experience, where legal gambling is popular, prostitution is legal in some counties, and marijuana sales and consumption are legal.

Disadvantage 1: Competition

The advantages of the US federal system are nonetheless balanced in part by several disadvantages. In many ways, competition among the states is healthy and produces better policy. Governors all want their states to have the best schools, the best roads, and the most attractive climate for new business. To achieve these goals, they try out new policies and adopt the policies of others. They develop partnerships with private industry to enhance economic opportunities for their residents and to attract more talent to their state.

But there is a destructive side to interstate competition as well. States frequently bid aggressively against one another for a new factory or facility by substantially lowering taxes, providing various costly subsidies, and in other ways lowering the revenues due to the state government. The state of Wisconsin, for example, has eliminated almost all taxes on manufacturing profits in an effort to attract more business—though critics deride such a practice as *corporate welfare*. Although many economists believe that competitive bidding and tax incentives have little impact on the ultimate decision of where to locate a business, few governors are confident enough to not at least enter the bidding.

When the massive online retailer Amazon.com announced plans to build a second distribution center somewhere in the United States—HQ2, as it became known—fierce competition developed among states to try to attract this business. With a promise of as many as fifty thousand employees working at the new facility, states understood that attracting HQ2 would generate billions of dollars for their local economies if they were chosen. States thus offered all kinds of financial and other inducements to attract HQ2, to the point that some experts determined that winning the competition would ultimately be more costly than beneficial to the state that Amazon.com picked. Ultimately, Amazon turned down massive incentive packages, such as the one worth $8.5 billion offered by Maryland, and chose to split its new headquarters into two locations: Arlington, Virginia, and New York City, New York. When some local leaders and citizen activists in New York City vigorously protested the incentives provided to Amazon, the company withdrew its offer to relocate there.

This disadvantage exists in many federal systems, but in some countries, such as Germany, taxes are set by the national government and apply everywhere. German states still compete for business in important ways, but they do not do so by lowering taxes on business. In the United States, competition actually can lower state taxes all the way to zero, as in Delaware, which has no corporate income tax. Many large financial institutions incorporate in Delaware to avoid taxes on business profits, and even international companies have found this US state to be a profitable tax haven. Moreover, US states generally do not want to have more generous social welfare benefits for the poor than neighboring states, and so they have engaged in a race to the bottom that results in less generous benefits for poor citizens. Although a few states have sought to implement creative new programs to deal with poverty, most have simply lowered benefits, hoping that in doing so they will not attract migration of welfare recipients to their state.

Disadvantage 2: Inefficiency

Centralized or more authoritarian-style governmental systems will always be more efficient in responding to crises, emergencies, and other short-term needs of citizens than a complex, multilayered federal system. Some of the most visible failures of the US federal system have occurred during natural calamities as federal, state, and local officials bickered over their respective responsibilities to respond.

In 2005, when Hurricane Katrina devastated the Gulf Coast states of Mississippi, Louisiana, and Alabama, the Federal Emergency Management Agency was slow to respond, and state and local officials failed to issue timely evacuation orders. The lack of

5. President George W. Bush (middle) discusses disaster relief with administrators of the Federal Emergency Management Agency. The agency's inadequacy in responding to Hurricane Katrina and other natural disasters is one shortcoming of a federal system.

coordinated response to the crisis left thousands of citizens vulnerable, many holed up in evacuation centers with no food or water, and many deaths were attributed to the failed government response.

In 2017, several massive storms caused severe flooding and damage in Texas, Florida, and especially Puerto Rico. Again, much controversy ensued over the responsibilities of different governments, with much of it focused on allegations of an inadequate federal response. Most telling, perhaps, was the reaction of President Trump to the criticism by local government leaders in Puerto Rico when he declared that the island government and its people should take more responsibility for their own plight and not expect the federal government to do everything for them. The president noted at one point the implications of the federal response for its own budget, thus making it clear that local governments would have to do more to finance the recovery effort.

6. Technical sergeant Heather Perez of the New Jersey Air National Guard (NJANG). After Hurricane Katrina, the NJANG flew a convoy to the gulf states region to transport medical support personnel.

Even during nonemergency situations, trying to forge cooperative arrangements among multiple governments is almost always difficult. A success story perhaps makes the point best. In 2017, the governments of the District of Columbia, Maryland, and Virginia each passed substantial expenditure increases to improve the deteriorating Washington metropolitan commuter train system. Each committed to act, but only if the others did as well. Political commentary marveled at the extraordinary accomplishment of regional cooperation among governments that had a long history of failing to work together.

Because states have no authority to influence national fiscal and monetary policy—because there is a common national currency regulated by the Federal Reserve Board—there exists no mechanism for state governors to coordinate state fiscal policies. States simply have no incentive to try to respond collectively to macroeconomic dislocations or other fiscal challenges, and the fiscal actions of states clearly have spillover effects on each other.

Disadvantage 3: Inequality

Compared to unitary systems and even many other federal systems, the US system tolerates a great deal of inequality. In the United States, the things that the government provides its citizens—public libraries, schools, roads, civil liberty protections—depend in large part on their location of residence. Many of the taxes citizens pay and the laws that they must obey also depend on the same.

Some states are quite wealthy and able to do much for their citizens, whereas others are very poor and severely constrained. Perhaps in no policy area are the inequalities across the country so apparent as in public education. Because the vast majority of funding of the public schools comes from state and local taxes, the disparities in educational resources, school facilities, support for teacher salaries, and other needs are substantial.

Vast differences in education can be seen without traveling very far. Some of the finest public schools in the country are in wealthy suburban communities of Fairfax County, Virginia, and Montgomery County, Maryland. But just a short drive away, in some areas of Washington, DC, the situation in the public schools is shockingly different, with facilities in disrepair, teacher salaries and support stagnant, and educational services that are common to most school systems in the United States lacking.

Although federal funding is one mechanism to help alleviate inequities among the states in such critical areas as education, national policy actions sometimes exacerbate the problem. In the 1980s, when the federal government wanted to recognize educational achievement, it created the designation Blue Ribbon Schools of Excellence. Schools apply for the prestigious designation, and studies show that the award has, not surprisingly, gone very disproportionately to schools in affluent communities. State and local governments tout the accomplishment of their Blue Ribbon schools, which has real impact on real estate market values in those communities as well as the ability to attract businesses eager to locate where families want to have access to the best schools. The admirable goal of creating an incentive for achieving excellence also had the effect of driving a greater distance between high-achieving and struggling schools.

Inevitably, there is inequality built into all federal systems, but many systems, such as those in Canada and Germany, try to minimize that problem as much as possible. In Germany, wealthier states pay into a fund that is distributed to poorer states. In this way, it is hoped that poorer states can in some way begin to catch up with wealthier states, by investing in infrastructure or schools.

In the United States, although some federal programs benefit poor states more than wealthy ones, on balance rich states get perhaps even more from the national government than poorer states do. States at or near the bottom of the socioeconomic ladder tend to stay there, regardless of federal largesse, although the wealthiest states have fluctuated a bit with the price of oil or food or other products.

Disadvantage 4: Accountability

A democratic republic is based on the principle of accountability: that citizens may reward or punish elected officials based on performance in office. That principle necessarily means being able to identify who is responsible for policy success and failure. A complex, multilayered federal system with thousands of governmental units makes this goal a real challenge. Citizens do not always know who is to blame when policies fail. Many Americans tend to look to the federal government as ultimately responsible for policy outcomes that have little or nothing to do with national-level action.

And then there are circumstances of a multilevel failure, as happened in 2014 when the discovery of lead-tainted drinking water sent the city of Flint, Michigan, reeling. For the average citizen, assigning blame was complicated: a local water authority had switched water sources for the city, causing the problem, but major budget cuts by the state government in oversight of water quality also contributed, and federal environmental water safety standards had not been enforced. All the while, for the better part of eighteen months, officials at all levels of government insisted that the water was not harmful to drink, a claim that turned out to be wrong. To many observers, it appeared to be a massive government cover-up or at least incompetence, but it was not easily apparent who was most responsible for the failure.

Federalism is far from a perfect system for the effective operations of government. It has substantial advantages, but they often are balanced out by policy failures that are not inherent to unitary systems. Going back to the founding era, there have been debates about the utility of a decentralized system with local autonomy and diverse policy outcomes throughout the country. And yet, for Americans, it is hard to imagine living under a different system altogether.

Chapter 7
Federalism in the world

The US government is the oldest continuing operating federal system, in large part because of its relatively high degree of stability and respect for the rule of law. But does that make the US system a model for other nation-states to emulate? Various scholars have described the US system as unique, unusual, or, more commonly, exceptional. But many other countries have federal systems, and their systems are also unique, and in some cases nations have designed their systems to avoid problems in the American model. Understanding those other federal systems helps us better recognize the strengths and weaknesses of the US system. And these other countries also offer institutions and policymaking systems worthy of emulation.

There are some two dozen countries with at least some degree of a federal structure. One study made a useful distinction between *mature* and *emergent* federations. In five continents (Europe, North America, South America, Australia, and Asia), there are mature federations, and in the sixth (Africa) there are some emergent federations. The federal systems of six countries— Switzerland (founded 1848), Canada (1867), Brazil (1889), Australia (1901), India (1950), and Nigeria (1999)—provide telling comparisons and contrasts.

Switzerland ("Swiss Confederation")

Switzerland became the second country to adopt a federal system of government with the adoption of its constitution in 1848. Prior to that, Switzerland operated as a confederacy of nineteen independent cantons. The creation of the federation followed a civil war between conservative Catholic and liberal Protestant cantons.

The Swiss constitution created a new federal nation out of the previously sovereign cantons. Somewhat similar to the US experience, the first experiment with federalism in Switzerland gave the national government very limited powers and reserved to the states the predominant amount of authority.

The US federalism example significantly influenced the development of the Swiss model, with the national government limited in power to certain core central functions such as regulation of foreign trade and tariffs, administering the postal service, and guaranteeing certain rights such as freedom of religion, the press, and association. The cantons held all powers not specifically granted to the central government in the constitution. The cantons could establish their own governmental systems, determine the breadth of independent powers for their communes (municipalities), organize their own judiciaries, and determine the level of direct democracy for their citizens. The cantons also controlled education, police forces, and levels of taxation, and even designated their own official language.

Again, somewhat similar to the United States, the constitution created a two-house Federal Assembly that consisted of a Council of States (Ständerat), composed of two deputies from each canton, and a National Council (Nationalrat), composed of two hundred representatives directly elected from the cantons, allocated in proportion to the population of each canton.

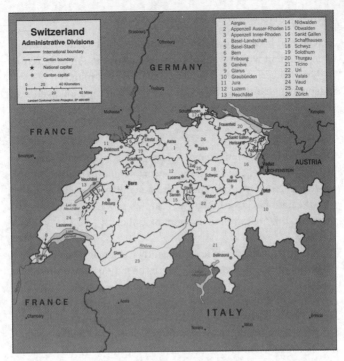

1	Aargau	14	Nidwalden
2	Appenzell Ausser-Rhoden	15	Obwalden
3	Appenzell Inner-Rhoden	16	Sankt Gallen
4	Basel-Landschaft	17	Schaffhausen
5	Basel-Stadt	18	Schwyz
6	Bern	19	Solothurn
7	Fribourg	20	Thurgau
8	Genève	21	Ticino
9	Glarus	22	Uri
10	Graubünden	23	Valais
11	Jura	24	Vaud
12	Luzern	25	Zug
13	Neuchâtel	26	Zürich

Switzerland
Administrative Divisions

——— International boundary
- - - Canton boundary
★ National capital
◉ Canton capital

7. **In 1848, Switzerland became the second country to adopt a federal system of government. In the Swiss system, cantons establish their own governmental systems, which in turn govern education, police forces, levels of taxation, and official languages.**

The Swiss constitution created an executive branch led by a federal council (Bundesrat) of seven members elected by the Federal Assembly. Each of the seven now leads one of the seven federal executive departments. The federal supreme court (Bundesgericht) had an appellate function regarding decisions of the cantonal courts, but no power to review the constitutionality of federal laws.

Switzerland, like the United States, strengthened its federal government powers over time. Switzerland twice has revised its constitution, in 1874 and in 2000. Most significantly, the 1874 constitution transferred some of the cantonal powers to the federal government, including raising an army, producing a common currency, and civil law. Another important change was to allow a simple majority at the national and cantonal levels to amend the constitution. In the United States, a constitutional amendment requires the support of two-thirds of each of the two houses of Congress and the consent of three-quarters of the states, and thus few proposed amendments succeed in passing. The Swiss constitution now has been amended more than a hundred times. The power of the federal judiciary expanded significantly through the amending process. The 2000 constitution expanded the federal power over financial systems and education and reaffirmed the continued sovereignty of the cantons. But cantons retain the power to levy taxes, administer schools, and decide what is taught and when.

Today, Switzerland has twenty cantons, six half cantons, and nearly three thousand communes. The two national legislative chambers have equal powers, and no federal bill becomes law unless enacted by both chambers. Voting systems in the Swiss cantons vary, but Switzerland, like many European nations, allows for national referenda.

Through referendum, Switzerland has navigated somewhat successfully one of the most vexing issues in federalism: unequal distribution of resources. In most federal systems, there are significant resource gaps between the wealthy and the poor subnational units. By the constitutional referendum in 2004, Switzerland empowered the federal government to balance inequalities among the cantons.

One of the challenges in comparing federal systems is that nations differ substantially in size, as well as in culture, geography, customs, and many other factors. Switzerland is a small country— less than sixteen thousand square miles, with a population of 8.2

million. In the United States, Wyoming is the least populous state, but it has more citizens than all but four of the Swiss cantons. The average Swiss canton has a population of a town like Garland, Texas, and five have populations of fewer than fifty thousand. As a result, neighboring cantons cooperate frequently, and in some cases cantons and the federal government enter into cooperative agreements. An example is education policy, traditionally the domain of the cantons but amended in 2006 to allow for federal–canton joint responsibility. Under this arrangement, Switzerland established a joint federal–cantonal council to manage higher education, with national standards of education set by the federal government and the cantons managing the operations of their jurisdictional universities. Although most public universities are managed at the cantonal level, two technical universities are managed by the confederation. Primary education remains with the cantons and the federal government regulates professional education.

Finally, the Swiss confederation has had to surmount linguistic and religious differences. Today, there are four national languages, with German, French, Italian, and Romansh spoken in different regions of the country. Attempts at forming federal systems in countries with different religious and ethnic groups have had mixed, mostly troubled outcomes, so Switzerland stands as an example for nations struggling with linguistic, religious, and, increasingly, ethnic cleavages.

Canada

The British North America Act of 1867 (later renamed the Constitution Act of 1867) united the provinces of Canada East (Québec), Canada West (Ontario), Nova Scotia, and New Brunswick and created the Dominion of Canada—the third oldest federation, after the United States and Switzerland. Great Britain wanted to unburden itself of supporting British Canada, and there also was fear of annexation by the United States that helped precipitate the move toward a stronger federation.

The framers of the Canadian constitution had the benefit of having observed the federal system to their south, in the nearly immediate aftermath of the US Civil War. That American tragedy convinced the Canadian constitution-makers of the necessity of a strong central government with a clear delineation of the federal–provincial division of power. In their view, the US federal system, with its long-standing debates over state sovereignty, was not a good model.

Under the Canadian constitution, the federal government's powers include full jurisdiction over trade and commerce, exclusive control over criminal law, the right to implement any form of taxation, the authority to enter into treaties with other nation-states, and control over the currency and national defense. The powers of the provinces, however, are substantial and include legislative control over hospitals, asylums, charities, municipal institutions, prisons, property, civil rights, and education. There also are concurrent powers that provinces share with the federal government, including those associated with agriculture and immigration. Any residual powers not specifically granted to the provinces are reserved to the federal government. Although the central government is quite powerful, the Canadian system in many respects is among the most decentralized federations in the world.

A good example of its decentralized operations is education policy. The national government plays almost no role, and the ten provinces and three territories generally run the education system and set their own curricula. As in the United States, there are school districts run by locally elected school boards. Those local school boards have the right to adapt the curriculum, and they have a great deal of autonomy in deciding how to distribute school funding. Canadians generally consider the public schools of high quality, and therefore far fewer children attend private schools in Canada than in the United States.

Canada is a federal monarchy with a parliamentary system similar to that of the United Kingdom. The national Parliament consists of the monarchy (and his or her federal representative, the governor general) and two legislative chambers, the House of Commons and the Senate. The monarchy, or Canadian Crown, is primarily ceremonial, handling the duties of head of state. Most of the federal power resides with the House of Commons and the executive council, consisting of the prime minister and cabinet (the heads of the executive departments). The number of seats in the House of Commons is proportional to the population of each province; however, special provisions allow provinces to have at least as many members of Parliament as senators, and grandfather clauses guarantee that some provinces have as many members of Parliament as they had in 1976 or 1985. The Senate is like the British House of Lords. Its members are regionally appointed and exercise considerably less power relative to the elected members of Parliament in the House of Commons. Regional appointment ensures adequate representation of the French-speaking linguistic minority, primarily located in the province of Quebec.

Each of the ten provincial governments is set up in a similar manner, with an appointed lieutenant governor representing the Crown as head of state, provincial elected legislatures, and provincial premiers and their executive councils. The provinces are no longer bicameral, however, having all abolished their senates (generally called legislative councils) because the provinces were largely cohesive and did not require the check on legislation by a coequal chamber. The three territories have their own governments but are under the authority of the federal government.

The constitution also created a strong federal judiciary, including the Supreme Court of Canada, which is the final referee of

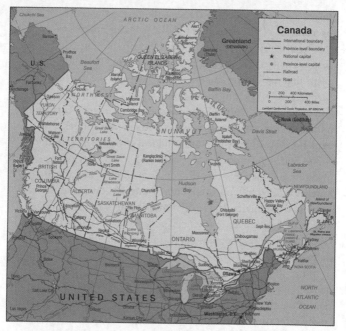

8. Canada, like most other populous nations, is a federal system. Since confederation in 1867, legislators have changed and expanded territories, resulting in the current union of ten provinces and three territories.

constitutional disputes between the federal and provincial governments. The Constitution Act of 1982 included the Charter of Rights and Freedoms (the Canadian equivalent of the US Bill of Rights) and gave the federal courts the power to strike down any federal or provincial law that violates charter provisions.

Although the United States and Canada are both decentralized federal systems, they are vastly different in structure and operation. Whereas the US Constitution enumerates certain limited powers to the national government and reserves the rest for the states, the Canadian counterpart reserves certain limited powers for the provinces and leaves the rest to the central government. Whereas the United States leaves matters of marriage, divorce, and most criminal law to the states, in Canada these are matters for the national government. This difference means that permitting same-sex marriage and the legalization of marijuana took place at the national level in Canada, although both began in the United States as state experiments. Gun policy in Canada also is national, whereas in the United States, regulation is primarily by state and local governments. In the United States, the national government's power to regulate interstate commerce is broadly construed, but in Canada, this power is limited to truly interstate, or international, commerce. But in both countries, the regulation of alcohol is heavily influenced by state and provincial government. Finally, Canadian education policy is far more decentralized than that in the United States.

One of the major challenges of Canadian federalism is that, unlike most of the thirty-six countries of the Organisation for Economic Co-operation and Development, municipalities are not allowed to tax income or sales, only property. Municipalities thus are not equipped to manage many of their greatest infrastructure, public transportation, and health needs, but must appeal to the provinces for financial relief with no assurance of receiving it. The federal government pays subsidies to the provinces, and both have the authority to tax income (personal and business) and sales. Because the population is shifting rapidly into increasingly financially burdened cities, Canadians debate whether the current system of fiscal federalism is the country's best approach to meeting the needs of its citizens.

Canadian federalism is somewhat asymmetric—for example, the constitution guarantees that three of nine supreme court justices must be from Quebec, and Quebec operates its own pension plan, whereas other provinces are covered by a national plan. Quebec's immigration and cultural policies are subtly different from those of the rest of the nation as well, in an effort to preserve Quebec's Francophone culture. In 1980 and again in 1995, the province voted against independence from Canada, in the latter case by an exceedingly narrow margin.

Like the United States, Canada is a large country, but unlike its neighbor to the south, Canada has a relatively small and highly dispersed population. At its founding, Canada was linguistically and religiously diverse, with a Protestant English-speaking majority and a Catholic French-speaking minority. The constitution of 1867 recognized this diversity and created a powerful central government while recognizing the importance of the provincial governments in preserving cultural distinctiveness.

Brazil

Federalism in Brazil historically has been complicated by the country's alternation between dictatorships and democracy. The country has had seven constitutions since 1824, the most recent written from scratch in 1988. The Brazilian federal system is multilayered, with a federal government, twenty-six states, a federal district, and more than five thousand municipalities.

Brazil first became a federal republic in 1889 after a military coup. The 1891 constitution declared a United States of Brazil modeled heavily after the US Constitution. But unlike the United States, Brazil did not create a federal structure to unite subnational units that had been largely sovereign; instead, the desire was to create better administrative control over a vast country. A military fiat and then a newly imposed constitution converted the former twenty-four provinces into semisovereign states. With a relatively weak national government, the governors of the two largest states, São Paulo and Minas Gerais, were able to dominate national affairs.

Until the 1930s, states governed themselves and had the authority to impose their own taxes, raise armies, and borrow money. State government debts were common, and the decentralized system proved to be highly unstable. In 1937, Brazil became a dictatorship, and the states lost their independent powers, until a military revolt in 1945 reestablished a federal democracy. Yet another military coup in 1964 centralized power again, with state governors appointed by the military. Brazil restored federalism again in 1985, and three years later created a federal constitution that remains in effect.

The new constitution gives states more power than they had before, including the right to draft their own constitutions. But over time, the national government has asserted dominance in policy initiation, and the supreme federal court has limited state autonomy by asserting the power of the national constitution. Like the US Constitution, Brazil's constitution reserves to the states all powers that are not granted to the federal government, while at the same time it establishes federal supremacy. But the Brazilian Supreme Court does not invalidate federal enactments for intruding on states' reserved powers. In addition, in Brazil the federal government has exclusive authority over several key policy areas, such as energy, communications and infrastructure, and fiscal and tax policy. Some national taxes are earmarked for states, and states collect their own version of value-added taxes as well as taxes on estates and automobiles. States have also borrowed from the national government and external sources.

The national government consists of a president; a bicameral legislature with a lower chamber (Chamber of Deputies), whose membership is allocated proportionally to the population size of each state, and an upper chamber (Federal Senate) composed of three elected members from each state; and a Supreme Court. Brazil directly elects its president, and if no candidate gets 50 percent of the vote, the top two candidates compete in a runoff election. Both chambers of the legislature overrepresent rural areas. In the lower chamber, for example, all states are entitled to at least eight legislators and the largest states are capped at seventy. Indeed, Brazil is second only to Argentina in the malapportionment of its upper chamber.

The responsibilities of state governments are defined in the national constitution, and all have the same structure and division of powers. Every state elects its own governor and unicameral legislature, and its governor then appoints a justice tribunal with the consent of the legislature. Different parties dominate in different states, but parties often form national and sometimes regional coalitions. The states have exclusive authority over public safety and metropolitan regions, however. Civil and criminal codes reside at the federal level and are uniform across the states.

In Brazil, the federal government generally initiates policy, but broad powers of implementation belong to the states. Brazil's federalism is fraught with financial challenges and vast inequalities between states in the north and the south. State economic autonomy has resulted in heavy borrowing from foreign countries and large debts, and the federal government has therefore tried to limit the power of states to borrow. Vastly unequal distribution of federal resources to the states has long been a sore point among many in the country. Today, the federal system in Brazil is teetering, as the country in 2018 turned to an authoritarian personality, Jair Bolsonaro, as its president; Bolsonaro has declared a need for much greater central control and expressed much admiration for past military dictatorship of the country and, thus, has alarmed proponents of a democratic Brazil with distributed powers.

Education policy in Brazil showcases the operation of its federal system. The 1988 constitution declares education a universal right that the government is responsible for promoting. The 1996 National Education Guidelines and Framework Law and subsequent legislation established nationalized standards for primary and secondary curriculum, the number of school days, evaluation of courses and schools, and a compulsory nine years of primary education.

At the federal, state, and municipal levels there are government education ministries and offices that have different responsibilities. Municipalities generally manage primary and secondary education under the federal requirements. The federal government regulates private educational institutions directly. There is a national Ministry of Education that drafts legislative language and provides financial and technical support to the subnational units managing the schools. A National Committee for the Evaluation of Higher Education supervises the system for assessing university courses and student learning. Federal public universities are considered the best in Brazil and are free of charge. Admission depends on performance on highly competitive entrance examinations. In 2009, the Ministry of Education established an official university entrance examination that is used by most universities but is not required, because some universities use their own entrance examinations.

Australia

After the arrival of the first fleet of British ships at Sydney Harbour in 1788, six self-governing British colonies evolved into what is now Australia. In 1901, after years of negotiations over creating a new federation, the six colonies of Australia approved a new constitution, and the British Parliament approved it via the Commonwealth of Australia Constitution Act of 1900. On enactment, the six colonies became states, joined later by three internal territories and seven external territories. Today, two of the three internal territories effectively function as states.

The federal system outlined in the Australian constitution borrowed largely from the American model, with powers divided between the national government and the states. The national legislative power is vested in a federal parliament consisting of the queen, a Senate, and a House of Representatives (collectively called the Parliament). The House of Representatives today consists of 150 representatives elected by the people from each state, with seats distributed in proportion to the state's population. The party controlling the House of Representatives chooses the prime minister and his cabinet. The seventy-six-seat Senate consists of twelve representatives democratically elected from each state, plus two from each of the two self-governing mainland territories. The Senate does not have power to initiate or amend money bills, but it does have the power to amend, fail to pass, or reject all other proposed laws coming from the House of Representatives.

What is somewhat different from the US model is the distribution of federal, state, and concurrent powers. Under the Australian constitution, the Parliament has exclusive power to impose excise taxes and to "make laws for the peace, order, and good government" of the nation. Other exclusive federal powers include regulating interstate trade and commerce as well as external affairs and "nationhood" powers such as defense, currency, and postal services. Concurrent powers include health, education, and taxation. In health policy, for example, Australian Medicare is funded by the federal government, yet service delivery happens at the state level, generally through state hospitals. All powers not specified in the constitution are reserved for the states. Further, the Australian constitution is extremely difficult to amend, requiring a majority of voters in a national referendum and a majority of voters in a majority of states (four of six) to pass. Perhaps as a result, the Australian constitution has been amended only eight times in Commonwealth history, the last time in 1977.

Formally, the distribution of powers in the constitution favors the states, although the balance of powers has over time shifted increasingly in a national direction. A 1920 High Court of Australia decision altered the balance strongly in a national direction when it declared that the existing constitutional assignment of powers was unworkable. The High Court effectively annulled the principle of "implied intergovernmental immunities"—that neither the national government nor the states could be affected by the laws of the other—and reserved state powers and thus gave the Commonwealth preeminence over the states. Notably, the High Court made it clear that the American model of federalism was not a legal basis for the construction of an Australian constitution. Further, the Commonwealth enacted the Income Tax Act of 1942, which gave it a monopoly on imposing income taxes. It did this by providing financial grants to states on the condition that they did not collect their own income taxes. The law was upheld in a High Court decision giving the Commonwealth the exclusive right to impose the income tax. Thus, through a series of High Court decisions, the Commonwealth achieved central fiscal control over state finances and stripped the states of most of their residual powers. Moreover, even in areas where states were delegated power, such as labor law, the national government has gradually preempted the states. In 2011, the national government passed consumer protection laws, replacing state and territorial laws.

States have their own parliaments and their own criminal laws, although the differences among them are not dramatic. It is harder to get alcohol and tobacco in New South Wales than in Victoria, and laws relating to drinking and driving differ across states. States differ in which crimes are punished by imprisonment and in the length of the terms, although federal laws regulate sentencing to some extent. States have their own laws regulating marijuana, but the national government legalized medical marijuana in 2016. Marriage and divorce are administered by the states, but Australia legalized same-sex marriages in 2017 after a postal survey showed more than 60 percent of Australians favored the change. States have their own constitutional law, which can be amended by referenda.

Federal systems are challenged by a variety of key factors, such as geographic size, population size, and diversity. Australia, like the United States and Canada, is a geographically large country, but like Canada and Switzerland, it has a relatively small population. Australia, unlike most of the Western democratic nations today, does not have linguistic and religious diversity challenges. Similar to many of the Western democratic nations, Australia has moved toward a federal system in which the balance of powers has become increasingly national, but where states and territories in some key policy areas still retain a great many responsibilities.

Education policy is one of the key areas of shared responsibility between the federal, state, and territorial governments. There is a national Department of Education and Training that provides partial funding of public schools and universities as well as some funding and regulatory support for early childhood education. It imposes few mandates, including a national curriculum for all schools and compulsory education until age seventeen. Otherwise, under the constitution, state and territorial governments have most of the responsibility for funding and administering education in Australia. Most funding of public schools comes from the states and territories, and these government units regulate both public and private schools, including school accreditation and student assessment, and they pay for infrastructure, maintenance, and teacher and administrator pay. Only about two-thirds of Australian students attend public schools, with the rest attending private and parochial education. Forty of Australia's forty-three universities are public, and the national government provides partial funding, based on student enrollments, as well as subsidized loan programs.

India

Britain ruled India from 1858 until 1947, and India became an independent nation with its own constitution in 1950. The constitution of India refers to the country as "a union of states" that would have at minimum a two-tiered system of governance. The constitution makes no mention of federation, although today there are three recognized tiers of government—the Union Government, the state governments, and the *panchyats* (village councils) and municipalities that, since 1991, have been constitutionally recognized as "institutions of self-government."

The constitution grants many exclusive powers to the federal government, including defense, energy, foreign affairs, High Court appointments, and levying of all taxes except sales taxes. There also are separate marriage and divorce laws for Hindus, Muslims, and Christians at the national level. The state legislative bodies have exclusive powers to make law in such areas as healthcare, land policy, electricity, and forming police forces. Concurrent powers exist over several policy areas, including criminal law, education, food policy, drugs, and economic planning. Residual powers not listed in the constitution are reserved to the national Parliament to legislate.

Parliament can amend major portions of the constitution without the participation of the states. The president appoints state governors, and the governors have the power to withhold assent to legislation passed by the state. Parliament can override state legislation for reasons of national interest. Parliament possesses exclusive power to form new states by separating territories from the existing ones, by uniting two or more states or parts of states, or by uniting any territory to a part of any state. Thus, the formal power distribution between the Union and states in India's federal system is highly asymmetric.

The Congress Party's dominance of Parliament and the state legislatures for about a quarter century maintained a system of a strong central government. The rise of new regional and state parties in the 1970s, followed by the defeat of the Congress Party in the 1977 parliamentary elections, eventually gave way to multiparty coalitions that focused their agendas on particular state-level needs. The coalition of many parties that defeated Congress in 1977 was called Janata, but it quickly split into the Janata Dal and the Samjwadi parties. With Janata's victory in 1977, many legislators simply changed parties to join the winning coalition. More recently, the Congress Party has splintered and spawned several regional parties that are loosely affiliated with Congress. For example, in Andhra Pradesh the Telegu Desam Party has advocated for the designation of that state as special category status, which in India's asymmetrical federalism would allow the state to receive a higher portion of national funds.

Today, India is a federal constitutional republic with a parliamentary system, twenty-nine states, and seven *union territories*, which are federal territories that have their own governments but are ruled directly by the central government. The Union Parliament is bicameral, consisting of a lower house, the Lok Sabha (House of the People), and an upper house, the Rajya Sabha (Council of States). The Lok Sabha has 543 members who are directly elected by the people from each state district, with district seats distributed in proportion to the state's population. The Rajya Sabha has 233 members, who are elected by the members of all the state legislative assemblies based on proportional representation. In this regard, the state governments, and not voters, select the upper chamber, as was initially true in the United States and remains true in Germany. As in the British Westminster system, the ruling party in the Lok Sabha elects the prime minister (the head of government) and Union cabinet.

The president of India is the head of state and is elected by an electoral college composed of members of both houses of Parliament and the state legislatures. The president of India has the power to scrutinize bills, make two appointments to the Lok Sabha (bringing the total number of members to 545), nominate 12 members to join the Rajya Sabha (bringing the total number of members to 245), and even dissolve the Lok Sabha. The *president's rule* in India allows the president to suspend a state government's powers and impose central rule in cases where there is civil unrest and the state is unable to function according to constitutional principles. This authority of the president gives the central government truly ultimate power over the states, and although it is intended for emergency situations, it has been misused by a ruling party to dissolve governments of states governed by an opposing party. This was especially common in the 1970s and 1980s, when Indira Gandhi evoked the president's rule fifty times. The president appoints not only the governors but also the lieutenant governors of the states for five-year terms, further solidifying central control. The federal judiciary has the power to invalidate any law or action that violates the constitution.

States have their own legislatures, which can be unicameral or bicameral. The appointed governor selects the chief minister and other ministers from the majority party coalition in the legislature. There are many national and regional parties, which form moderately stable coalitions at the national level, but these coalitions may vary from state to state. State laws differ to some extent; twenty states with large numbers of Hindus have limits on killing or selling cows, but nine states have no such laws. In contrast, three states with large Muslim populations ban the sale and consumption of alcohol. State police enforce state law and constitutional rulings, but are not required to cooperate with the national government and may not share intelligence or give assistance in controlling insurgencies or anti-Muslim violence.

Education policy authority is divided between the national, state, and local governments. The constitution establishes free and compulsory education for ages six to fourteen as a fundamental right. There is a national Department of Education that develops educational standards and instructional materials and designs textbooks, but the states are not required to follow national plans and usually design their own educational curricula, choose their own textbooks, and have their own school boards. As in the United States, some states have rewritten their history books to fit the narrative preferred by the state government. The federal Department of Education allocates some funding to the states, although the states themselves provide the majority of the funding. There are state-level education ministries that oversee and coordinate educational programming at the local levels. State education ministries and municipal governments jointly administer the urban government schools. In the rural areas, a district board or village council oversees school operations. India has a large private education system as well, with nearly one-third of students in private schools. Government heavily regulates the private schools' curricula and operations, thus minimizing the differences between public and private education in the country. Although the federal government has established higher-education standards, it has little control over a large number of for-profit institutions that operate outside the regulatory framework and conduct unaccredited programs.

One of the great challenges of federalism in India is that the country is geographically large, with a commensurately large population. It is linguistically, culturally, religiously, ethnically, and economically highly diverse. The country recognizes twenty-two national languages, and states have their own official languages. Tensions between Hindus and Muslims have frequently led to violence, and there are important divisions on caste as well. The centrally focused federal constitution in part is intended to hold the country together and prevent state secession and civil war. Although the power relationship between the Union government and state governments is highly asymmetric, with the rise of regional and state parties, the states have been able to exert substantial influence over federal legislation in the bicameral Parliament.

Nigeria

Nigerian federalism has its antecedents in the colonial era of British rule. In 1914, Britain established northern and southern protectorates to allow the British to better supervise, control, and govern the country. In 1954, the colonial authority established a more formal federal system composed of a national government and three regional ones: eastern, western, and northern. By the end of the decade, each of the three regions became self-governing, and national independence followed in 1960. The independence constitution maintained a federal system, as did the republican constitution of 1963, which added another regional government. The country experienced a coup and a counter-coup and pogroms against the Igbo people living in the northern region, many of whom fled to the eastern region. The president then announced a new regional division into twelve states, which created three eastern states and would deprive the Igbo of most of the petroleum in the east. The eastern region then declared itself the independent state of Biafra (which lasted until 1970), resulting in a civil war that lasted three years. After the war, the number of states gradually expanded to the current thirty-six. But until 1999, Nigeria had only the appearance of a federal system and was instead governed by military leaders who bought the loyalty of tribal groups through channeling financial resources to regions and to individuals.

The origin of modern Nigerian federalism traces back to the 1999 constitution, which established a presidential system of government as well as the formal relationship among the Federal Capital Territory, the thirty-six states, and the local governments. The National Assembly is a bicameral body, with a Senate composed of two members from each state and a 360-member House of Representatives elected by simple majority vote in single-member districts. The president is directly elected by the people, and his or her powers dwarf those of the other branches of government.

The 1999 constitution identifies powers that are exclusive, concurrent, and residual to the states. Among the powers exclusive to the federal government are defense, foreign affairs, commerce, telecommunications, immigration, and customs and excise taxes. But it is the control of crude oil production that gives the federal government tremendous power over the regional and local government units. The federal government controls the distribution of the oil revenues, which are divided monthly among the subnational units, and it is this financial dependence on the federal government that makes the subnational units truly subservient. Federal distribution decisions have been highly contentious and the cause of regional conflict as well as calls by the states for more autonomy to generate their own revenues. Additionally, the Nigerian police agency is centralized, headed by a presidentially appointed inspector general of police, and there are no state police agencies. State governors and legislatures have little power in matters of policing and enforcing laws. There are currently calls in Nigeria for the creation of state police, but it is not clear whether this will materialize or what effect it might have on policing.

States have elected governors, unicameral legislatures, and a judiciary appointed by the governor and confirmed by the legislature; like the national government, they are generally dominated by their executives. Governors are in charge of infrastructure and the provision of services, such as roads, schools, water, and public health. Some state budgets are larger than the budgets of countries such as Kenya, and in many states there is widespread corruption in elections and government administration.

Education policy illustrates the complexities of federalism in Nigeria. There is a federal Ministry of Education that oversees educational operations in the country, but the states establish most of the educational curriculum and administrative requirements. Local authorities additionally have substantial discretion in implementing the state-controlled policies. This loose configuration means that there is enormous variation in educational operations and quality across the country, with very little success at developing unified policies at the national level.

The federal government does have a Universal Basic Education Commission that mandates a free and compulsory nine-year period of formal schooling (six years primary and three years secondary). At the university level, the Ministry of Education funds and manages directly a few colleges in each of the thirty-six states. Therefore, all teachers and staff of these colleges are federal employees. Admission to the colleges is based in part on performance on a nationally standardized entrance examination.

Nigeria recognizes some 371 tribes, but 78 percent of the population belongs to one of the four largest tribes, all of whom have members in other African countries. What makes African federalism distinct is that many states are dominated by a single tribe. For example, the Yoruba tribe dominates the population of eight Nigerian states, and Yorubaland—the cultural region of the Yoruba people—encompasses these states and also parts of Benin and Togo. Igboland encompasses seven states and a portion of an eighth. Tribalism poses its own challenges in a federal system given the allegiance of members primarily to a tribe and the separation that occurs between peoples of the different tribes. Developing consensus within governing boundaries is not easy when various groups generally interact only with other group members and do not understand the perspective of persons from other tribes. The country is also divided by religion, with Muslims slightly outnumbering Christians in most recent surveys. In some states and tribes, Muslims and Christians coexist in peace, but there has been considerable religious violence in recent years because nine northern states have adopted sharia civil and criminal law, as have portions of three other states. These states have imposed penalties such as floggings, amputations, and death by stoning.

Federalism

Nigeria is a relatively large country—about twice the size of the US state of California, and it is very populous, with about 186 million people. It is the one federal nation defined as emergent rather than mature. The legacy of British central control and then military control of the country has complicated the implementation of a federal system with truly decentralized authority.

The many paths to federalism

A single country profile from each region of the world cannot convey the full range of complexities of federal systems, and there are significant differences even within these regions. The linguistic cleavages in Switzerland are mirrored in Belgium but not in Germany, which has important religious and cultural differences among the states. Although Nigeria and South Africa both face similar problems with tribal divisions and resource distribution, the former has a legacy of tribal conflict and civil war, and the latter had a legacy of apartheid and the powerful personality of Nelson Mandela, who was critical in helping the country avoid civil war. India's federal system faces many of the same linguistic and ethnic cleavages as Pakistan, but the two federal systems depart in important ways, and both differ from the federal monarchy in Malaysia, which is more centralized, and from that in Australia, where linguistic and religious cleavages are virtually nonexistent. In the Americas, Canadian federalism is different from that of Mexico, and Brazilian federalism differs from that of Argentina.

Nations take varied paths to federalism and confront different problems. Four of the nations profiled here were, like the United States, once British colonies, and another was a colony of Portugal. Some deal with a dazzling array of ethnic groups and languages; others have important religious and regional cleavages. Some have long histories of democracy; others have had repeated periods of military rule. The path that each has taken to federalism has shaped the system that emerged. In the United States, the history of independent colonies revolting against a central government was a factor in the creation of a decentralized system. In South Africa, in contrast, the creation of tribal homelands called Bantustans served the apartheid government in cementing segregation and aiding in the dominance of the white regime. This, in turn, led to a strong suspicion of a decentralized version of federalism as the constitution was drafted. There is no one blueprint for federalism, and all countries can learn from the experiences of others.

The precise nature of any nation's federal system is continually contested by different social, economic, and political groups that seek to gain advantage of changes in the system and by advocates for national uniformity or local autonomy in various policy areas. In all federal countries there are voices for more national standards in education and for federal control of the curriculum and other voices that call for more local autonomy of curriculum. In each country the balance is slightly different, but in nearly all federal systems the regional governments are left to build schools, administer schools, hire teachers, and implement curricula. But in Nigeria, the national government has taken increased responsibility for building schools, often without consulting regional or local governments, allowing the government to claim credit for advances in education.

In many countries there is some debate over what should be taught in sex education classes and in what grades. In Nigeria, the national government mandated an abstinence-only sex curriculum, but allowed some states to remove certain words or images from the curriculum. The emphasis has been on preventing the spread of HIV/AIDS. In Mexico, the national government chose a set of textbooks in 2006 that acknowledged different sexualities and openly discussed masturbation, despite strong objections from religious conservatives. In Canada, the provinces choose their own sex education curriculum, and there are substantial differences in the ages at which various topics are introduced and the way that the topics are discussed. In India, although the national government has recommended some form of sex education, most states do not include the topic at all in their curriculum. In the United States, there has been a spirited debate between conservatives who argue that sex education should seek primarily to discourage sexual activity and those who argue that full sexuality education is needed. The national government has at times offered money to the states to implement abstinence-only sex education programs, and many of the most conservative states offer this type of program. However, even with federal money available, many states refused to limit their sex education curriculum.

The politics of federalism in most countries are complicated, and frequently factions take different positions regarding federal authority, depending on the issues being debated and whether groups will benefit more from national or local control. Also, opinions about the desirable degree of national authority as opposed to greater local control may well change with the political balance of power.

In the United States, for example, liberals have traditionally argued for stronger national uniformity of business and environmental regulations, and conservatives have argued for a small federal role and greater state autonomy in those issues. But when Republicans have control of the federal government, they often seek to preempt states from bolstering their economic regulations, while Democrats champion the rights of states to innovate with stricter regulations. Even in the area of sex education, the social conservatives in the United States who advocated for a national program in abstinence-only education were more generally opposed to national education programs, except in this single-issue area. When conservatives in Mexico lost their battle to substantially alter the national sex education curriculum, they then sought greater state autonomy in curricular matters. Federalism is constantly evolving everywhere, as actors see advantages in different arrangements.

In the end, the idiosyncratic elements of each nation's federalism are a function of the social, economic, and political forces that contest politics; the nature of the ethnic, linguistic, political, and other cleavages; and the decisions made in the past by leaders. Although some countries, such as Nigeria, do completely reshape their federal systems over a relatively short period of time, more commonly federal structures are dependent on paths taken long ago.

An American model for the world?

Academics, government officials, leaders of nongovernmental organizations, and youth leaders who come to the United States, as well as those abroad, have many questions about the US system. Not surprisingly, one of the most common questions is whether we believe the US system is workable in their country or in other countries. The answer that we give is no. The US system is far from perfect and did not prevent a bloody civil war some seven decades into the country's history. Moreover, the American political system is adapted to US political realities, not to the challenges facing other countries. For example, the US federal system would work differently if implemented in Kenya, where states would likely be tribal homelands. Nothing in the US federal system is adapted to deal with the multitude of languages in India and Pakistan or the long-standing linguistic cleavage in Belgium. The democratic nature of the United States makes it a poor exemplar for the United Arab Emirates.

To be sure, there are aspects of the US federal system and the experiences of its operations that provide useful lessons, as with aspects and experiences of federalism in other countries. We support efforts by the US government to invite community and political leaders, academics, and journalists, among others, to the

United States to learn about the federal system and its operations. At the same time, it is useful for Americans to visit other federal systems to see different possible solutions to the challenges that the United States faces.

What often attracts international visitors to the US system is its longevity. Federalism is doubtless one part of the explanation for how a powerful country can successfully operate with a constitution drafted more than 230 years ago. Nonetheless, federalism in the United States has changed dramatically over this period and continues to evolve, particularly with the national government's role having become so much more powerful than the founders of the Republic could have anticipated. Moreover, developments in the late 2010s, most noteworthy the rise of a populist fervor among a significant minority that favors authoritarian control, leave us less sanguine about the future of American federalism than we were when we began lecturing on this topic to international visitors some thirty-five years ago.

By the end of the Bill Clinton administration, the intensified political polarization at the national level was beginning to seep more deeply than ever into state and local politics. With the election of Donald J. Trump as president, attacks on basic democratic processes have reached a level unthinkable to most Americans in even the recent past. Political thinkers and leaders across the political spectrum now worry about the long-term stability of American governing institutions.

The challenges to American democracy are echoed by the rise of populist and nationalist leaders across the world—in Brazil and India, Turkey and Russia, the Philippines and Hungary, among others. These leaders profess admiration for each other and offer each other support. In 2019, President Trump entertained Brazilian president Jair Bolsonaro in Washington, DC, and expressed admiration for his presidency, even as the Brazilian leader has expressed admiration for his country's past military dictatorship. The new and emerging authoritarian leaders threaten to undermine the legitimacy of elections and of the courts, and they attack the media. These are worrying times for federal and nonfederal systems alike. The US federal system has enabled the country to endure longer than any other democratic system, but it is not foolproof. Institutions can be robust, but bad leaders can weaken the best of them.

These events challenging the foundations of US democracy bring us back to where we started—with the ideals and practices of the system themselves. Are current problems in American democracy the result of a flawed system? Americans are not accustomed to asking that question. Surely the longevity and stability of a governing system are evidence of its sound institutional structures. But yet, the union hung by a thread more than 150 years ago and survived only because of the bravery of troops in a long series of bloody battles. It was not inevitable then that the system would survive, nor is there any such guarantee today.

References

Preface

Paraphrasing Charles O. Jones, derived from his book *The Presidency in a Separated System*, 2nd ed. (Washington, DC: Brookings Institution Press, 2005), 1.

Chapter 2: Federalism, American style

On the US Articles of Confederation: "Articles of Confederation: March 1, 1781," Avalon Project at the Yale Law School, http://avalon.law.yale.edu/18th_century/artconf.asp; Jack P. Greene, "The Background of the Articles of Confederation," *Publius* 12, no. 14 (Autumn 1982): 15–44; James E. Hickey Jr., "Localism, History and the Articles of Confederation: Some Observations about the Beginnings of U.S. Federalism," *Ius Gentium* 9 (2003): 5–24; Calvin H. Johnson, "Homage to CLIO: The Historical Continuity from the Articles of Confederation into the Constitution," *Constitutional Commentary* 20, no. 3 (2003–2004): 463–514; Donald S. Lutz, "The Articles of Confederation as the Background to the Federal Republic," *Publius* 20, no. 1 (Winter 1990): 55–70; Samuel B. Payne Jr., "The Iroquois League, the Articles of Confederation, and the Constitution," *The William and Mary Quarterly* 53, no. 3 (July 1993): 605–20; Douglas G. Smith, "An Analysis of Two Federal Structures: The Articles of Confederation and the Constitution," *San Diego Law Review* 34 (1997): 249–342.
On the US Bill of Rights: Garrett Epps, "The Bill of Rights," *Oregon Law Review* 82 (2003): 517–29.

On the origins of US federalism in the Constitution: Martin Diamond, "What the Framers Meant by Federalism," in *American Intergovernmental Relations: Foundations, Perspectives, and Issues*, ed. Laurence J. O'Toole and Robert K. Christensen, 96–105 (Washington, DC: Congressional Quarterly Press, 2013).

On US federalism in the nineteenth century: Daniel Elazar, "Federal–State Cooperation in the 19th Century United States," *Political Science Quarterly* 79 (June 1964): 248–81.

Chapter 3: The evolution of federalism in law

Ware v. Hylton, 3 U.S. 3 Dall. 199 (1796).

Marbury v. Madison, 5 U.S. 1 Cranch 137 (1803).

Fletcher v. Peck, 10 U.S. 6 Cranch 87 (1810).

Martin v. Hunter's Lessee, 14 U.S. 1 Wheat. 304 (1816).

McCulloch v. Maryland, 17 U.S. 4 Wheat. 316 (1819).

Cohens v. Virginia, 19 U.S. 6 Wheat. 264 (1821).

Gibbons v. Ogden, 22 U.S. 9 Wheat. 1 (1824).

Wabash, St. Louis and Pacific Railway Company v. Illinois, 118 U.S. 557 (1886).

Texas v. White, 74 U.S. 7 Wall. 700 (1869).

National Labor Relations Board v. Jones & Laughlin Steel Corporation, 301 U.S. 1 (1937).

United States v. Darby Lumber Co., 312 U.S. 100 (1941).

Wickard v. Filburn, 317 U.S. 111 (1942).

United States v. Lopez, 514 U.S. 549 (1995).

United States v. Morrison, 529 U.S. 598 (2000).

Brown v. Board of Education of Topeka, Kansas, 347 U.S. 483 (1954).

Plessy v. Ferguson, 163 U.S. 537 (1896).

Cooper v. Aaron, 358 U.S. 1 (1958).

Loving v. Virginia, 388 U.S. 1 (1967).

Obergefell v. Hodges, 576 U.S. _____ (2015).

South Dakota v. Dole, 483 U.S. 203 (1987).

Chapter 4: What state and local governments do

Reynolds v. Sims, 377 U.S. 533 (1964).

"Don't Worry, You're in Safe Hands," quoted in John Myers, "Who's Governor of California? This Week, It's Not Jerry Brown," *Los Angeles Times*, July 25, 2016, http://www.latimes.com/politics/

la-na-pol-sac-acting-governor-rules-california-20160726-snap-story.html#.
Bush v. Gore, 531 U.S. 98 (2000).

Chapter 5: Fiscal federalism

Projection of federal aid to states in 2019: White House, "Aid to State and Local Governments," https://www.whitehouse.gov/wp-content/uploads/2018/02/ap_14_state_and_local-fy2019.pdf.

Chapter 6: Advantages and disadvantages of federalism

Roe v. Wade, 410 U.S. 113 (1973).

Chapter 7: Federalism in the world

For an analysis that makes the distinction between mature and emergent federations: Ronald L. Watts, *Comparing Federal Systems*, 3rd ed. (Montreal: McGill–Queen's University Press, 2008).

For studies that describe the Swiss federal nation and the powers of the cantons: Thomas Fleiner, "The Current Situation of Federalism in Switzerland," *REAF* 9 (October 2009); Kurt Nuspliger, "Federalism in Switzerland" (Paper for the Panel on Comparative Federalism Constructing Tomorrow's Federalism Conference, Regina, Saskatchewan, Canada, March 25–26, 2004),http://www.forumfed.org/library/federalism-in-switzerland/.

For studies that describe the Canadian federal system: Johanu Botha, "All You Need to Know about Canadian Federalism," *Spectator Tribune*, April 16, 2013, https://spectatortribune.com/everything-you-always-shouldve-known-about-canadian-federalism/;
John D. Richard, "Federalism in Canada," *Duquesne Law Review* 44 (Fall 2005): 5.

On the Brazilian Supreme Court having no power to invalidate federal enactments that intrude on state-reserved powers:
Keith S. Rosenn, "Federalism in Brazil," *Duquesne Law Review* 43 (2005): 585.

On federalism in Brazil: Edward L. Gibson, ed., *Federalism and Democracy in Latin America* (Baltimore: Johns Hopkins University Press, 2004).

State economic autonomy in Brazil has resulted in heavy borrowing and debts: Edward L. Gibson, ed., *Federalism and Democracy in Latin America* (Baltimore: Johns Hopkins University Press, 2004), 19.

On federal powers in Australia: Brian Galligan, "Parliament's Development of Federalism" (Research Paper No. 26 2000–01, Department of the Parliamentary Library, June 2001); Bhajan Grewal and Peter Sheehan, "The Evolution of Constitutional Federalism in Australia: An Incomplete Contracts Approach" (CSES Working Paper No. 22, Melbourne: Centre for Strategic Economic Studies, November 2003); Greg Taylor, "Federalism in Australia," *University of Monash Law Research Service* 11 (2010), http://classic.austlii.edu.au/au/journals/UMonashLRS/2010/11.html.

Indian municipalities as "institutions of self-government," quoted in Ronald L. Watts, *Comparing Federal Systems*, 3rd ed. (Montreal: McGill–Queen's University Press, 2008), 37.

Indian parliament has exclusive power to form new states: M. Govinda Rao and Nirvikar Singh, "Asymmetric Federalism in India" (UC Santa Cruz International Economics Working Paper No. 04-08, April 2004), 3.

On the rise of multiparty coalitions in India: Forum of Federations, "Federalism in India and the World," http://www.forumfed.org/library/federalism-in-india-and-the-world/.

On some states in India rewriting school textbooks: Shreya Roy Chowdhury, "BJP's Major Achievement in Rajasthan: Rewriting School Textbooks to Reflect RSS Worldview," https://scroll.in/article/901001/bjps-major-achievement-in-rajasthan-rewriting-schools-textbooks-in-the-rss-worldview.

On a description of Nigeria pre-1999 as governed by military leaders: Ronald L. Watts, *Comparing Federal Systems*, 3rd ed. (Montreal: McGill–Queen's University Press, 2008), 50; Ladipo Adamolekun, "Introduction: Federalism in Nigeria," *Publius* 21, no. 4 (Autumn 1991): 1.

Description of the Nigerian National Assembly: Ronald L. Watts, *Comparing Federal Systems*, 3rd ed. (Montreal: McGill–Queen's University Press, 2008), 50.

Control of crude oil gives Nigerian national government tremendous power over subnational units: Osisu Ta, "Federalism in Nigeria: A Critique," *Journal of Political Sciences & Public Affairs* 3, no. 3 (2015): 1.

Federal revenue distribution decisions in Nigeria are highly contentious: Ronald L. Watts, *Comparing Federal Systems*, 3rd ed. (Montreal: McGill–Queen's University Press, 2008), 51.

On "emergent" versus "mature" federal systems: Ronald L. Watts, *Comparing Federal Systems*, 3rd ed. (Montreal: McGill–Queen's University Press, 2008), iv.

Further reading

Anderson, George. *Fiscal Federalism: A Comparative Introduction.* New York: Oxford University Press, 2010.

Beer, Samuel H. *To Make a Nation: The Rediscovery of American Federalism.* Cambridge, MA: Belknap Press of Harvard University Press, 1993.

Burns, Nancy. *The Formation of American Local Governments: Private Values in Public Institutions.* New York: Oxford University Press, 1994.

Chemerinsky, Erwin. *Enhancing Government: Federalism for the 21st Century.* Stanford, CA: Stanford University Press, 2008.

Conlan, Timothy J. *From New Federalism to Devolution: Twenty-Five Years of Intergovernmental Reform.* Washington, DC: Brookings Institution Press, 1998.

Conlan, Timothy J. *New Federalism: Intergovernmental Reform, from Nixon to Reagan.* Washington, DC: Brookings Institution Press, 1988.

Elazar, Daniel J. *American Federalism: A View from the States.* 3rd ed. New York: Harper & Row, 1984.

Elazar, Daniel J. *The American Partnership: Intergovernmental Competition in the Nineteenth Century United States.* Chicago: University of Chicago Press, 1962.

Elazar, Daniel J. *Exploring Federalism.* Tuscaloosa: University of Alabama Press, 1987.

Elkins, Stanley, and Eric McKitrick. *The Age of Federalism: The Early American Republic, 1788–1800.* New York: Oxford University Press, 1993.

Gerston, Larry N. *American Federalism: A Concise Introduction.*
Armonk, NY: Sharpe, 2007.

Gibson, Edward L., ed. *Federalism and Democracy in Latin America.*
Baltimore: Johns Hopkins University Press, 2004.

Grodzins, Morton. *The American System.* Chicago: Rand McNally,
1974.

Jones, Charles O. *The Presidency in a Separated System.* 2nd ed.
Washington, DC: Brookings Institution Press, 2005.

Karmis, Dimitrios, and Norman Wayne, eds. *Theories of Federalism: A
Reader.* New York: Palgrave Macmillan, 2005.

Ketcham, Ralph. *The Anti-Federalist Papers and the Constitutional
Convention Debates.* New York: Signet Classics, 1993.

Kincaid, John. "Federalism and Rights: The Case of the United States
with Comparative Perspectives." In *Human Rights: Current Issues
and Controversies,* edited by Gordon DiGiacomo, 83–113. Toronto:
University of Toronto Press, 2016.

LaCroix, Alison L. *The Ideological Origins of American Federalism.*
Cambridge, MA: Harvard University Press, 2010.

Menon, Anand, and Martin A. Schain, eds. *Comparative Federalism:
The European Union and the United States in Comparative
Perspective.* New York: Oxford University Press, 2006.

Nagel, Robert F. *The Implosion of American Federalism.* New York:
Oxford University Press, 2001.

Peterson, Paul E. *The Price of Federalism.* Washington, DC: Brookings
Institution Press, 1995.

Peterson, Paul E., Barry G. Rabe, and Kenneth K. Wong. *When
Federalism Works.* Washington, DC: Brookings Institution, 1986.

Robertson, David. *Federalism and the Making of America.* New York:
Routledge, 2012.

Rodden, Jonathan A. *Hamilton's Paradox: The Promise and Peril of
Fiscal Federalism.* New York: Cambridge University Press, 2006.

Ryan, Erin. *Federalism and the Tug of War Within.* New York: Oxford
University Press, 2011.

Seymour, Michael, and Alain-G. Gagnon, eds. *Multinational
Federalism: Problems and Prospects.* New York. Palgrave
Macmillan, 2012.

Shapiro, David L. *Federalism: A Dialogue.* Evanston, IL:
Northwestern University Press, 1995.

Singh, Mahendra Prasad, and Veena Kukreja, eds. *Federalism in
South Asia.* New York: Routledge, 2014.

Urofsky, Melvin I., ed. *Documents of American Constitutional and Legal History: From Settlement through Reconstruction*. New York: Knopf, 1989.

Walker, David B. *The Rebirth of Federalism: Slouching toward Washington*. 2nd ed. Washington, DC: Congressional Quarterly Press, 1999.

Watts, Ronald L. *Comparing Federal Systems*. 3rd ed. Montreal: McGill–Queen's University Press, 2008.

Further reading

Index

Note on index: For the benefit of digital users, indexed terms that span two pages (e.g., 52–53) may, on occasion, appear on only one of those pages. Page references followed by a "*f*" indicate figure.

C

Index